SUNDAY SCHOOL TEACHERS AND SMALL GROUP LEADERS:

You can use this study for any age group, from high school to seniors, and for new members or new believers classes.

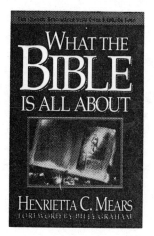

To use this study, you and your students will need copies of the classic *What the Bible Is All About* or *What the Bible Is All About, Quick Reference Edition* by Henrietta Mears. These best-selling books provide an easy-to-understand yet detailed overview of the entire Bible.

You will also want to get a copy of *The Big Picture Bible Time Line,* which is frequently referred to in this guide. It is a useful resource that will make your teaching more visual and more effective.

PASTORS:

You can also use this study as a framework for a 5- to 10-sermon series overview of the Bible.

The Bible is one book, one history, one story, His story. Behind the 10,000 events stands God, the Builder of history, the Maker of the ages. Eternity bound the one side, eternity bounds the other side, and time is in between: Genesis—origins; Revelation—endings; and all the way between, God is working things out. You can go down into the minutest detail everywhere and see that there is one great purpose moving through the ages: the eternal design of the Almighty God to redeem a wrecked and ruined world.

— From *What the Bible Is All About* by HENRIETTA MEARS

The Bible, the greatest document available for the human race, needs to be opened, read and believed. *What the Bible Is All About* will help make the reading and study of God's Word interesting, challenging and useful. We commend it to you.

— BILLY AND RUTH GRAHAM

GROUP STUDY GUIDE

WHAT THE BIBLE IS ALL ABOUT

A 5- TO 10-WEEK JOURNEY FROM GENESIS TO REVELATION

EDITED BY WES HAYSTEAD

Gospel Light
Living Word Curriculum
Ventura, California, U.S.A.

PUBLISHING STAFF

Wes Haystead, Editor
Kyle Duncan, Editorial Director
Gary S. Greig, Ph.D., Senior Editor
Virginia Woodard, Assistant Editor
Lee Torrence, Designer

NOTE: Sections of this manual are adapted from *Highlights of
Scripture,* a study series originally developed by Henrietta Mears.

HOW TO MAKE CLEAN COPIES FROM THIS BOOK

YOU MAY MAKE COPIES OF PORTIONS OF THIS BOOK IF:

- You (or someone in your organization) are the original purchaser.

- You are using the copies you make for a noncommercial purpose (such as teaching or promoting a ministry) within your church or organization.

- You follow the instructions provided in this book.

HOWEVER, IT IS *ILLEGAL* FOR YOU TO MAKE COPIES IF:

- You are using the material to promote, advertise or sell a product or service other than for ministry fund-raising.

- You are using the material in or on a product for sale.

- You or your organization are **not** the original purchaser of this book.

By following these guidelines you help us keep our product affordable.

Thank you,

Gospel Light

CONTENTS

CONTENTS

INTRODUCTION

WHAT THIS COURSE IS ABOUT

God's Word is vibrant and alive, and His plan for our lives is contained between the pages of *His* book—the Bible. Everything we need to know about living in wholeness is contained within the pages of His Word. Yet, we sometimes forget that the Bible is more than a series of unrelated, independent books—it is a connected, all-encompassing, interwoven work that provides a panoramic view of His love and plan for us.

However, the average person knows little about the Bible. Very few have a comprehensive idea of the whole book. We need, besides a microscopic study of individual books, chapters and verses, a telescopic study of God's Word in order to better understand His plan of salvation and movement in our lives. Through this study, you and your group will be able to see the interconnection between the Old and New Testaments, between the prophets and Christ. You will also trace the bloodline of the Messiah as you travel through Genesis to Revelation.

In this course, we are going to take the equivalent of a five- to ten-week plane trip, viewing the six highest peaks of God's revelation. In each week's lesson, we will fly to a new peak (except in Session 1, when we will "visit" two peaks) and gain a better perspective of His plan and His hand in shaping history. As we complete our panoramic survey of His Word, we will have the opportunity to draw closer to Him through a clearer understanding of the Bible and His deep, abiding love for His children.

The Bible is a book of 66 books written by at least 40 authors over a period of about 1,600 years. To help us gain an accurate perspective of this monumental work, we will be using the best-selling Bible study resource *What the Bible Is All About* by Henrietta Mears. This book provides helpful summaries of each book in the Bible, helping us see the common threads of Good News from beginning to end.

As we begin this exploration, we must keep in mind that sometimes the Bible gives a great deal of detail, while at other times there are only very brief statements. However, gaining the perspective of the Bible's major peaks provides a helpful mental map in which to locate and understand the great riches the Book contains.

"The Bible is one book, one history, one story, His story. Behind the 10,000 events stands God, the builder of history, the maker of the ages. Eternity bounds the one side, eternity bounds the other side, and time is in between: Genesis—origins, Revelation—endings, and all the way between, God is working things out. You can go down into the minutest detail everywhere and see that there is one great purpose moving through the ages: the eternal design of the Almighty God to redeem a wrecked and ruined world" (*What the Bible Is All About* by Henrietta Mears, page 20).

IT'S YOUR CHOICE IN USING THIS COURSE

This exciting study of Scripture highlights has been designed to fit a variety of learning situations:

- **You have a choice of two outstanding textbooks.**
- **You have a choice of course length (from 5 to 10 sessions to as many as 52 sessions).**
- **You have a choice of session plans (from 60 minutes to more than 2 hours).**
- **You have a choice of settings (classroom or home), meeting times (Sunday mornings, Sunday evenings, weekdays or evenings) and frequency (once a week, every day or night, weekend retreat).**
- **You have a choice of age groups: adults or, with some adaptation, older teenagers. (For tips on how to teach this course to older teens, see "Giving Teenagers a Bible Overview" on page 79.)**

Whenever or wherever you can get a group of people together to give them a panoramic overview of their Bible—this manual will be an invaluable guide.

A CHOICE OF TWO TEXTS

What the Bible Is All About has been a best-selling Bible study resource for 40 years, selling more than 3,000,000 copies! The *What the Bible Is All About: Quick Reference Edition* is a simplified, graphic version intended for those with limited Bible backgrounds, reading skills, and/or time available for study. The two books differ significantly in their formats, but they each give a clear, concise overview of every book in the Bible. They also provide valuable background information on the writers and main characters, giving informative views into Bible history and culture.

Why should your students secure one of these texts? Making sure that each class member has a copy of either text is valuable insurance that what is learned in this course will not be quickly forgotten. The goal is not just to give an overview of historical periods, nor to improve ability to locate the books of the Bible. The real value of this course will come throughout the remainder of each person's life as they are better equipped to read, study and understand God's Word. *What the Bible Is All About* is an invaluable companion for many years of productive Bible study!

As teacher, you may choose which of these versions would be most appropriate for the group you are going to teach—or you may want to give the class participants their choice. In addition, either or both texts will be helpful resources for you as you prepare to teach each lesson.

THE LEADER'S GUIDE

This leader's guide is a unique companion to *What the Bible Is All About* and *What the Bible Is All About: Quick Reference Edition*, offering a stimulating and enjoyable opportunity for group study of the highlights of Scripture.

This leader's guide is unique because it:

- Offers the flexibility of completing an overview of Scripture highlights in either five or ten sessions;
- Is based on the premise that a study of Bible highlights is a truly exciting adventure of great value for everyone: adults (and teens), novices and scholars, believers and seekers, male and female;
- Organizes the vast span of Bible history into six periods, has three to five major events for each period, and the key characters for each event;
- Provides useful handles for looking into the meaning of historical events, identifying the greatest fact and the greatest truth for each period of Bible history;
- Includes a comprehensive One-Year Bible Study Plan for individual study or group study after completing the course overview;
- Provides suggestions for adapting the course to fit the needs and interests of teenagers;
- References *The Big Picture Bible Time Line*, an innovative resource, which allows you to place around your room a complete visual panorama of Bible history. (Suggestions are made for various ways to use the *Time Line*, including the points when specific pages should be displayed.);
- Requires very few additional supplies for class sessions. (An overhead projector is helpful, but not necessary. Blank paper, index cards, pencils, felt markers are typical of the easily secured materials, which help add variety and stimulate involvement. Suggested supplies are listed at the beginning of each session.);
- Suggests individual reading assignments to review each session, adding further reinforcement to each person's learning.

SESSION PLAN

Each of the five sessions is flexibly designed to be completed in one of three major time schedules:

1. Five sessions of 60-75 minutes each.
2. Five sessions of more than 75 minutes each.
3. Ten sessions of 60 minutes each.

NOTE: Groups desiring a longer study should refer to the instructions for a "One-Year Bible Study Plan" beginning on page 63.

- **SESSION KEYS.** Each session has specific goals of its own, called Session Keys. This section highlights the key verse, key idea and key resources for the session. Preparation guidelines are also included in each session.

- **SESSION AT A GLANCE.** This practical tool gives a visual overview of each session, allowing the leader to better prepare for dynamic teaching. It shows the three different teaching time frames available to the leader, the various portions of each session, and how much time is required to complete each session component.

- **SESSION PLAN/LEADER'S CHOICE.** The session plan presents the choices for flexibility in teaching the course. As the leader, you have some choices for completing the course and each session. Two important symbols are used in the session plans to aid in extending each lesson over two separate sessions.

- **GETTING STARTED.** Each session begins with a choice of two get-acquainted, relationship-building activities, which also help group members capture the big picture of the scope of Bible content.

 This symbol indicates the **Two-meeting track,** which allows you to extend the session over two meetings, giving group members more time for discussion. The stop-and-go sign means to **END** your first meeting and **BEGIN** your second meeting at the point where the symbol appears in the session plan. Each of the five sessions in this manual can thus be easily made into two complete sessions, for a total of 10 sessions (Time schedule 3).

 You will find instructions placed in boxes and marked with this clock symbol. This information provides optional learning experiences to extend this session over two meetings or to accommodate a session longer than 60-75 minutes (Time schedules 2 or 3).

- **GETTING INTO THE WORD.** Each session contains three to five major points, enabling class members to recall the major events of each period of Bible history. Complete instructions are given to enable the teacher to guide class members in helpful and enjoyable learning experiences.

- **GETTING PERSONAL.** Each session concludes with instructions and questions for summarizing session highlights, helping people make personal application of a main truth, and suggestions for individual study.

A FEW TEACHING TIPS

1. Keep It Simple. The Bible contains a vast amount of highly interesting, deeply meaningful information. Avoid trying to pass all this information on to your eager learners. They will remember far more if you keep the focus on the big picture: the Six Mountain Peaks of Bible History, major events, characters, facts and truths.

2. Keep It Light. Some of the introductory activities in this manual are fun! This is intentional. Many people who most need this course are intimidated by the scope of the Bible. Often there is fear that their biblical ignorance will be exposed. People who are intimidated and fearful are not ready to learn. The games, the Bible books poem, *The Big Picture Bible Time Line* are all devices to help people relax so they can learn efficiently—and to keep the various repetitions of reviewing highlights from becoming boring.

3. Keep It Significant. Because this is a survey course using some light touches does not mean its content can be handled frivolously. Keep clearly in mind—and repeatedly emphasize to your class—this course is dealing with the major events and issues of God's dealings with men and women.

4. Keep It Interactive. The learning activities in this manual provide a variety of involving experiences, recognizing the various learning styles that will be present in any group of adults. Although some of the activities may not fit your preferred style, by using this varied path to learning you make sure that those who learn differently than you do will have their needs met. The most common type of involvement is using the Bible, locating, reading and talking about selected passages. If you have people in your group who are unfamiliar with the locations of Bible books, your patient encouragement will help them make giant strides in developing skill in working with the structure of the Bible.

NOTE: Two helpful techniques aid people in locating Bible references. First, and most common, is to use the contents page in the front of the Bible. Second, holding the Bible in one hand, open to the middle. Most of the time you will be in Psalms. When you divide the first half of the Bible in half again, you will usually be in 1 Samuel. Dividing the second half of the Bible in half usually brings you to Matthew. Subdividing the Bible in this manner helps a person move quickly to the section being sought.

5. Keep It Prayerful. Both in your preparation and in each class session, pray earnestly that you and your class will learn what the Lord wants you to learn from His Word. A personal relationship with the Author is necessary to properly understand Scripture (John 5:39,40).

REPRODUCIBLE HANDOUTS FOR *WHAT THE BIBLE IS ALL ABOUT*

The Six Mountain Peaks of Bible History

The Bloodline of the Messiah

The Periods of Bible History Outline

The Bible—A Library of Smaller Books

Kings and Prophets Chart

What Does the Bible Say About...?

THE SIX MOUNTAIN PEAKS OF BIBLE HISTORY

Creation to Call of Abraham

Call of Abraham to Coming Out of Egypt

Coming out of Egypt to Coronation of Saul

Coronation of Saul to Captivity in Babylon

Captivity in Babylon to Christ

Christ to Consummation of All Things

THE BLOODLINE OF THE MESSIAH

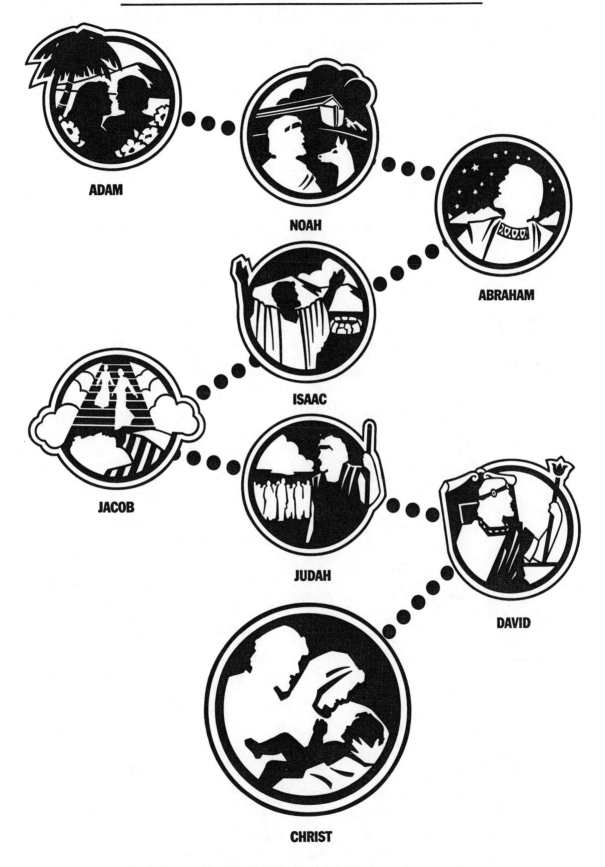

ADAM

NOAH

ABRAHAM

ISAAC

JACOB

JUDAH

DAVID

CHRIST

THE PERIODS OF BIBLE HISTORY OUTLINE

PERIOD	PEOPLE	EVENTS	SCRIPTURE
1. Creation to Call of Abraham	Adam & Eve Noah	1. Creation 2. Fall and Promise 3. Redemption 4. Flood 5. Judgment of Babel	Genesis 1–11
2. Call of Abraham to Coming out of Egypt	Abraham Isaac Jacob Joseph Job	1. Call of Abraham 2. Preparation of Jacob 3. Descent into Egypt	Genesis 12–50 Job 1–42
3. Coming out of Egypt to Coronation of Saul	Moses Joshua The Judges: Deborah Gideon Samson Samuel	1. Exodus from Egypt 2. Giving of the Law 3. Wilderness Wanderings 4. Conquest of Canaan 5. Judges Rule the Land	Exodus 1–18 Exodus 19–Leviticus Numbers–Deuteronomy Joshua Judges–1 Samuel 7
4. Coronation of Saul to Captivity in Babylon	Saul David Solomon Rehoboam Jeroboam Hezekiah Isaiah Jeremiah	1. Kingdom United 2. Kingdom Divided 3. Downfall of the Kingdom	1–2 Samuel 1 Kings 1–11 1 Chronicles 2 Chronicles 1–9 1 Kings 12– 2 Kings 23 2 Chronicles 10–35 2 Kings 24, 25 2 Chronicles 36
5. Captivity in Babylon to Christ	Daniel Ezekiel Nebuchadnezzar Ezra Nehemiah Esther	1. Capture Under Babylon 2. Restoration Under Persia 3. Hellenistic Rule 4. Seleucid Kings 5. Maccabean Independence 6. Roman Rule	Ezekiel/Daniel Obadiah Ezra–Esther Haggai–Malachi The Intertestamental Period
6. Christ to Consummation of All Things	John the Baptist Jesus Christ Twelve Apostles Paul	1. The Coming of Christ 2. The Church 3. Consummation of All Things	Gospels Acts/Epistles Revelation

THE BIBLE — A LIBRARY OF SMALLER BOOKS

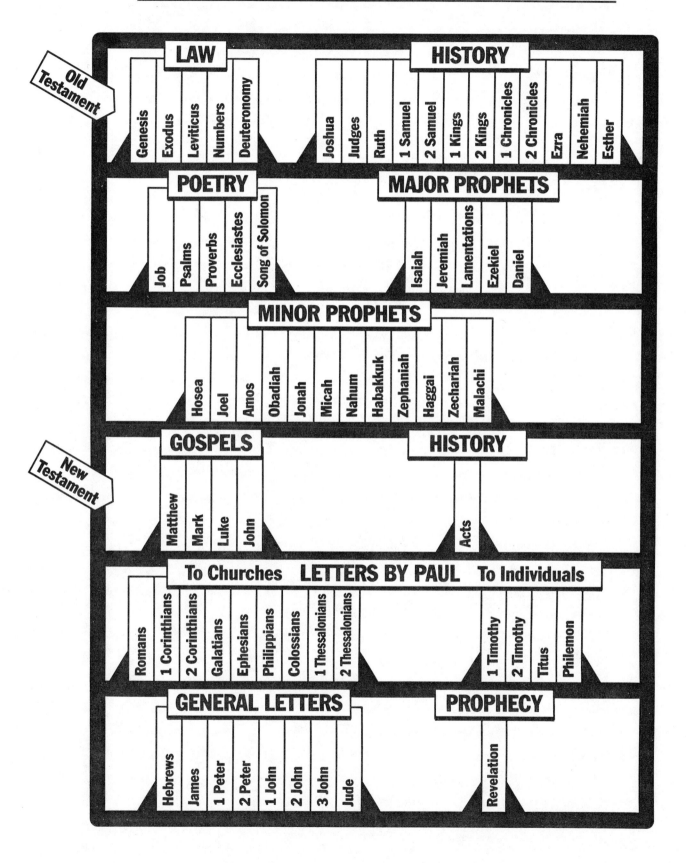

Old Testament

LAW
Genesis, Exodus, Leviticus, Numbers, Deuteronomy

HISTORY
Joshua, Judges, Ruth, 1 Samuel, 2 Samuel, 1 Kings, 2 Kings, 1 Chronicles, 2 Chronicles, Ezra, Nehemiah, Esther

POETRY
Job, Psalms, Proverbs, Ecclesiastes, Song of Solomon

MAJOR PROPHETS
Isaiah, Jeremiah, Lamentations, Ezekiel, Daniel

MINOR PROPHETS
Hosea, Joel, Amos, Obadiah, Jonah, Micah, Nahum, Habakkuk, Zephaniah, Haggai, Zechariah, Malachi

New Testament

GOSPELS
Matthew, Mark, Luke, John

HISTORY
Acts

LETTERS BY PAUL
To Churches: Romans, 1 Corinthians, 2 Corinthians, Galatians, Ephesians, Philippians, Colossians, 1 Thessalonians, 2 Thessalonians
To Individuals: 1 Timothy, 2 Timothy, Titus, Philemon

GENERAL LETTERS
Hebrews, James, 1 Peter, 2 Peter, 1 John, 2 John, 3 John, Jude

PROPHECY
Revelation

KINGS AND PROPHETS CHART

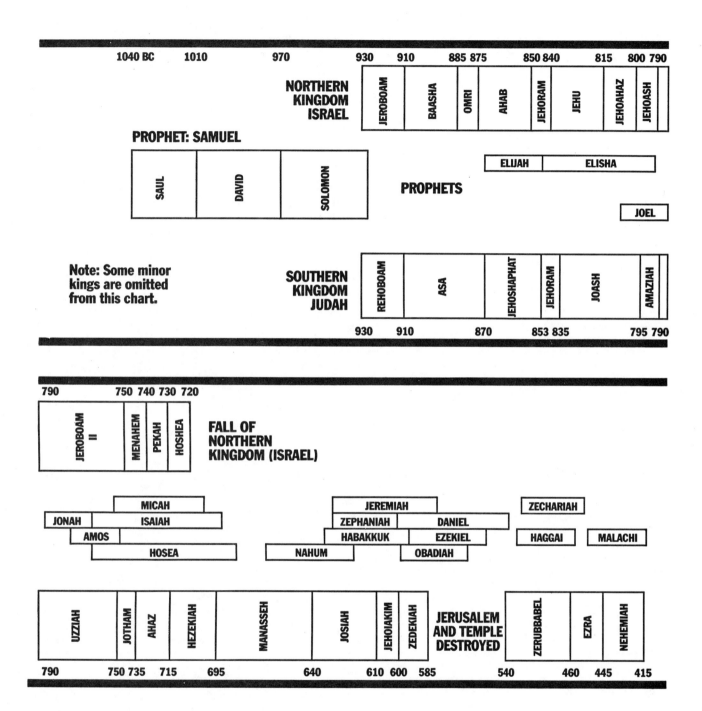

WHAT DOES THE BIBLE SAY ABOUT...?

The existence of God?—Genesis 1:1; Exodus 3:14; Psalm 14:1

The meaning of life?—Ecclesiastes 12:8,13,14; John 10:10

Life after death?—Romans 6:23; Hebrews 9:27

Other ways to heaven?—John 3:36; 14:6; Acts 4:12

The value of the individual?—Genesis 1:26,27; Luke 12:7

Real love?—1 Corinthians 13:4-7,13

The existence of evil?—Romans 1:21,22; Galatians 5:19-21

Getting along with people?—Philippians 2:3,4; James 4:1-3

Friendship?—Proverbs 17:17; 18:24; John 15:13-15

Marriage?—Genesis 2:24; Proverbs 5:18; 18:22; Matthew 19:9

Success?—Jeremiah 9:23,24; 17:7,8; Matthew 20:25-28; Mark 8:36

Guilt?—Isaiah 1:18; 1 John 1:9

Loneliness?—Psalm 145:17,18; Matthew 28:20; John 14:18

Grief?—Psalm 34:18; 1 Thessalonians 4:13,14; 1 Peter 5:7

Worry?—Deuteronomy 31:6; Isaiah 26:3; Matthew 6:25-27,34; John 14:1-3;
Philippians 4:5,6

Jesus?—John 14:6; Colossians 1:15-17; 1 Timothy 2:5; 1 John 5:12

Church?—John 13:35; Romans 12:4-8; 1 Corinthians 12:4-13,27-30; 14:1,12;
Ephesians 2:19-22; 4:11-13; Hebrews 10:25; 1 Peter 4:10,11

The Bible?—Psalm 119:9-11,105; 2 Timothy 3:16; Hebrews 4:12

The power of Satan and the spirit world?—Luke 10:17-20;
Romans 8:38,39; 2 Corinthians 2:10,11; Ephesians 4:26,27; 6:10-18;
Colossians 1:13,14; 1 Peter 5:7,8

PERIOD OF THE PATRIARCHS

BEGINNING THE BLOODLINE OF CHRIST

Creation to Call of Abraham
Call of Abraham to Coming out of Egypt

S·E·S·S·I·O·N · K·E·Y·S

▌KEY VERSE

"Abram believed the Lord, and he credited it to him as righteousness." Genesis 15:6

▌KEY IDEA

Humanity fell when Adam and Eve believed the serpent instead of God. Humanity is restored by walking in faith with the Lord.

▌KEY RESOURCES

■ Genesis 1–50; Job 1–42

■ Selected New Testament references

■ Chapters 1, 2,15 in *What the Bible Is All About* and/or chapters 2, 3,19 in *What the Bible Is All About: Quick Reference Edition*

■ *The Big Picture Bible Time Line*

PREPARATION

Provide blank name tags and felt pens. Make a tag for yourself.

On each of six sheets of poster board, letter a different period of Bible history:

- Creation to Call of Abraham
- Call of Abraham to Coming out of Egypt
- Coming out of Egypt to Coronation of Saul

- Coronation of Saul to Captivity in Babylon
- Captivity in Babylon to Christ
- Christ to Consummation of All Things

Mount the six posters (in sequence) around the room.

On a table at the front of the room, provide masking tape and materials for one of these Getting Started choices:

1. Choice 1: Index cards, felt pens.
2. Choice 2: Pages from *The Big Picture Bible Time Line*.

Copy "The Six Mountain Peaks of Bible History" and "The Bible—A Library of Smaller Books" pages (11 and 17) for each person. Also make an overhead transparency of the pages and "The Periods of Bible History Outline." Secure an overhead projector and focus it at the front of the room. (If you don't have an overhead projector, simply pass out copies to the group.)

Have ready sheets of blank paper (1 sheet per 4-5 people) and felt pens.

CHRIST'S BLOODLINE

ADAM   **NOAH**   **ABRAHAM**

SESSION 1 AT A GLANCE

SECTION	ONE SESSION PLAN		TWO SESSION PLAN	WHAT YOU'LL DO
Time Schedule	60 to 75 Minutes	More than 75 Minutes	60 Minutes (each session)	
Getting Started	10	10-20	*Session One:* **20**	Focus on the Big Picture in Scripture
Getting into the Word	45	65-80	40	Learn Major Persons and Events of the Period
Step 1	15	20	20	Step 1—Creation and Fall
Step 2	15	20	20	Step 2—Flood and Judgment
			Session Two Start Option: **10**	
Step 3	15	25	**25**	Step 3—Abraham, Isaac, Jacob
(Step 4 option)	(15)	(15)	15	(Step 4 Option—Joseph)
Getting Personal	5	5-10	10	Apply Basic Truths to Your Life

S·E·S·S·I·O·N · P·L·A·N

LEADER'S CHOICE

Two-meeting Track: This session is designed to be completed in one 60-75 minute meeting. If you want to extend the session over two meetings and allow group members more time for discussion, **END** your first meeting and **BEGIN** your second meeting at the stop-and-go symbol in the session plan.

The boxes marked with the clock symbol provide optional learning experiences to extend this session over two meetings or to accommodate a session longer than 60-75 minutes.

GETTING STARTED (10 minutes)

CHOICE 1 — SIX PERIODS OF BIBLE HISTORY

Welcome people as they arrive and guide them to complete and wear a name tag. Invite them to letter on an index card the name of a Bible character they feel is interesting or one they don't know anything about. Each person then greets one other person, tells one interesting fact about the character on the card, then exchanges cards. People continue meeting each other, exchanging facts and cards. (Be prepared to suggest some characters and simple facts to anyone who feels "stuck.")

As additional people arrive, greet them and involve them in this activity until you give a signal (ring a bell, flash the lights, stop the music, etc.). When you have everyone's attention, call attention to the six posters and instruct everyone to take the card they now have and tape it to the wall next to the appropriate poster. Assure people that it is "legal" to seek assistance from others if they have ended up with a name they do not know well.

CHOICE 2 — BIBLE TIME LINE

Welcome people as they arrive and guide them to complete and wear a name tag. Invite them to choose a *Bible Time Line* page from the stack. (If you have a large class, you may have people work in pairs, sharing a page between them. It is not necessary for every page to be used in this get-acquainted activity.)

Each person then greets one other person, and determines if between the two of them they know one interesting fact about the *Time Line* page, then exchanges pages. People continue meeting each other, exchanging facts and pages. As additional people arrive, greet them and involve them in this activity until you give a signal (ring a bell, flash the lights, stop the music, etc.). When you have everyone's attention, call attention to the six posters and instruct everyone to take the page they now have and tape it to the wall next to the appropriate poster. If wall space is limited, some pages may be taped above or below others.

Whichever choice you used, give an official welcome and introduce the course.

The average person knows little about God's Word, the Bible. Very few have a comprehensive idea of the whole book. Besides a microscopic study of individual books, chapters and verses, we need a study of the big view of Scripture. We are going to take the equivalent of a (five-ten, etc.) weeks' plane trip, viewing the mountain peaks of God's revelation.

Show "The Six Mountain Peaks of Bible History" transparency or refer to the handout as you distribute copies to group members.

The six peaks on this sketch make the major divisions of the Bible very clear. We will be using these peaks as reference points as we seek to gain an overview of the total Bible and its central message. This is no simple task, as the Bible is a book of 66 books written by at least 40 authors over a period of about 1,600 years. To help us gain an accurate perspective of this monumental work, we will be using the well-known Bible study resource *What the Bible Is All About* by Henrietta Mears. This book provides helpful summaries of each book in the Bible, helping us see from beginning to end the common threads of God's good plan for men and women through Christ.

As we begin this exploration, we must keep in mind that sometimes the Bible gives a great deal of detail, while at other times there are only very brief statements. For example, Genesis 1–12 covers a longer period of time than from Genesis 12 to the birth of Christ! Also, Exodus 1 covers centuries while Exodus 2 through the next three books (Leviticus, Numbers, Deuteronomy) covers only 40 years. Obviously we cannot divide the Bible evenly by chapters or even by time spans if we want a balanced summary of the great acts of God. However, gaining a perspective of the Bible's major mountain peaks provides a helpful mental map in which to locate and understand the great riches the Book contains. This session will explore the first two peaks: *Creation to the Call of Abraham* and *Call of Abraham to Coming out of Egypt*.

 GETTING STARTED OPTION: UNDERSTANDING THE BIBLE (20 minutes) This option will add 10 minutes to the end of the Getting Started section.

Show "The Bible — A Library of Smaller Books" transparency or refer to the handout as you distribute copies of the page to the group. Present a brief summary of the structure of the Bible, showing the cohesion of its central message.

Old Testament (39 books): An Account of a Nation
Message: "The Savior Is Coming!"

- **Law (5 books)**
- **History (12 books)**
- **Poetry (5 books)***
- **Prophecy (17 books: 5 Major Prophets, 12 Minor Prophets)***

* Lamentations is a poetical book, which is placed in the middle of the Major Prophets. Some lists vary in the number of Poetry and Prophecy books depending on how Lamentations is classified.

New Testament (27 books): An Account of a Man
Message: "The Savior Has Come!"

- **Gospels (4 books — the Life of Jesus)**
- **History (1 book)**
- **Letters/Epistles (21 books: 9 to churches by Paul, 4 to individuals by Paul, 8 general)**
- **Prophecy (1 book)**

Read aloud this quote by Henrietta Mears (page 20 in *What the Bible is All About*) to emphasize the united message of the total Bible: **"The Bible is one book, one history, one story, His story. Behind the 10,000 events stands God, the builder of history, the maker of the ages. Eternity bound the one side, eternity bounds the other side, and time is in between: Genesis — origins, Revelation — endings, and all the way between, God is working things out. You can go down into the minutest detail everywhere and see that there is one great purpose moving through the ages: the eternal design of the Almighty God to redeem a wrecked and ruined world."**

GETTING INTO THE WORD (45 minutes)

Step 1 — Creation and Fall

Step 2 — Flood and Judgment

Step 3 — Abraham, Isaac and Jacob

Step 4 (OPTIONAL) — Joseph

STEP 1 — CREATION AND FALL
(15 minutes)

PERIOD 1/EVENT 1—CREATION

Introduce this first part of the first period:

The first period covers the events from Creation to the call of Abraham. This story is told in the first twelve chapters of Genesis, yet it covers a span of at least 1,600 years. There is no certain chronology of this opening age, and scholars disagree in efforts to compute the figures of this period. The Bible is not intended to be an all-inclusive record of the history of either the natural world, the human race, or ancient civilizations, but a record of what God did in human history starting with the creation of the world and the first man and woman.

Divide the class into four sections. Assign each section one of the following Scriptures. People work individually or in pairs to find and read their assigned passage in order to answer this question: **What does the Bible tell us of the Creator and of His Creation?**

> Genesis 1:1-5
> Genesis 1:26-31
> Job 26:10-14
> John 1:1-4

Allow a minute or two for people to locate and read their assigned passage. Then invite volunteers to share their answers. Be prepared to add comments that clarify or expand as needed:

Creation as recorded in Genesis 1 begins with the God of creation; first with the fact of His existence, then immediately with the acts of His creation. God is mentioned 34 additional times between Genesis 1:1–2:3, the first account of creation. As you look over the order of creation, notice that the sequence moves from the inanimate to the animate, from the lower to the higher. Notice also that each day's creation prepared the way for God's next creative act, all leading to the crowning act of creation, the making of man, a creature after God's own image and likeness.

A more detailed description follows in chapter 2, and many other creation passages appear throughout Scripture. Job (a book of poetry that explores the question of suffering and the goodness of God and fits chronologically between Genesis and Exodus) focuses on God's great power. John goes back beyond the beginning, giving a glimpse of the very nature of God, a Being who communicates and speaks to us, His creation.

EVENT 2—HUMANITY'S FALL

Transition into the next major event:

The next event of importance is the Fall. If the classical evolutionary theory were correct, humanity should by now have shown marked improvement in every area of life. In spite of the passage of thousands of years, and the supposed advances of civilization, any newspaper is full of evidence that people are no nearer perfection today than were Adam and Eve.

Assign four more passages to the same four sections of your class. Instruct them to answer, **How does the Bible explain the spoiling of a world God had created and pronounced "good"?**

> Genesis 3:1-7
> Genesis 3:8-13
> Genesis 4:6-10
> Romans 5:12-14

Allow a few moments for people to read and think, then invite volunteers to share their answers. Respond to the answers people give.

Satan appeared in a fascinating way and tempted Adam and Eve to doubt God's wisdom and love. As a result of their sin, their eyes were opened. Every time a person sins, the same experience is repeated. Everyone deals with:

- the same God and His loving, all-wise laws;
- the same tempter;
- the same kind of appeals;
- then disobedience;
- then conscience reveals the inadequacies and shortcomings.

The destructive path of sin is vividly shown right in the family of the first couple. Angry and jealous feelings push Cain to deceive ("Let's go out to the field," Gen. 4:8) and then murder his own brother.

Paul describes the terrible chain reaction that began with the sin of Adam and Eve. Sin and death became entwined in the life of all men and women, not because of God's laws, but because of the pervasiveness of sin throughout humanity and in each person's life.

EVENT 3 — THE PROMISE OF REDEMPTION

Present this brief overview of God's promise of redemption from the Fall.

As a result of disobedience, humanity was in a terrible predicament. Sin brought condemnation, death, separation from God, and there was nothing people could do to resolve the problem. God did not delay in beginning to reveal his marvelous plan of salvation. In Genesis 3:15, even before announcing the consequences of Adam and Eve's sin, He gives the first promise of the Redeemer: The offspring (seed) of the woman will crush Satan. This is the beginning of a "scarlet thread," which weaves through the entire Bible, tying together a long series of God's merciful actions to restore His creation—culminating in the death of His Son, Jesus.

Bible Time Line: page 1 (Creation/Adam & Eve—The Fall)

OPTION *(20 minutes)*
This option will add 5 minutes to the Step 1 section.

Ask for volunteers to read aloud the following verses, which expand our understanding of humanity's plight and God's plan. Comment briefly on each one to make sure the point is clearly made.

John 1:4,5 (From the beginning, God's light has penetrated the darkness, offering hope even when people have resisted Him.)

Romans 3:10,11,23 (Sin infects us all. None can claim to be free of its corruption.)

Romans 6:23 (From the beginning, sin has produced death, while God has always offered life.)

STEP 2 — FLOOD AND JUDGMENT
(15 minutes)

EVENTS 4 AND 5 — THE FLOOD AND JUDGMENT AT BABEL

Invite group members to explore two great judgments and promises that followed the Fall.

Divide the class into small groups of four or five each. Assign each group one of the following passages. Instruct them to read their verses, then work together to write a concise caption for that passage expressing judgment and/or promise. For example, a caption for the story of the Fall could be, "Disobey and Pay—God's Light Shows What's Right."

Genesis 6:9-14
Genesis 7:5-12
Genesis 7:20-24
Genesis 11:1-4
Genesis 11:5-9

Give each group a sheet of blank paper and a felt pen. Allow several minutes for groups to read and then plan and write their caption. Invite a volunteer from each group to show their caption and explain what they feel it describes about the verses they read. Comment briefly after the captions have been shared:

The Flood was the judgment for men and women's deliberate and constant evil on the earth. Notwithstanding the darkness and sinfulness of these people, God did not send His punishment without first giving them warning through Noah, the preacher.

Humanity had a fresh start after the Flood, but soon failure was repeated. They were determined to "make a name" for themselves. God judged their arrogance by confusing their one speech into many languages, resulting in their being "scattered" over the earth.

Assign each of the groups a New Testament reference about Noah to discover what Jesus and the Early Church taught about God's judgment and promise through the Flood.

Luke 17:26,27 (God will again judge the world for its sin.)

Hebrews 11:7 (Faith in God's promise brings escape from judgment.)

1 Peter 3:20 (God is both patient and resolute in administering judgment and in providing salvation.)

2 Peter 2:5,9 (God has proven that He judges the ungodly and protects the righteous.)

After groups have had time to read their passage and discuss the New Testament view of the Flood, invite volunteers to share their insights.

Bible Time Line: page 2 (Noah's Ark—The Flood)

OPTION *(20 minutes)*
This option will add 5 minutes to the Step 2 section.

Summarize the first period of Bible history (Creation to Call of Abraham):

The Greatest Fact: God is Creator and Ruler of All (Genesis 1:1)

The Greatest Truth: Redemption Through Sacrifice (Genesis 3:15,21)

The redemption of a fallen race through the death of an innocent substitute is introduced in God's act of clothing Adam and Eve. Before the skin could be used for a covering, an innocent lamb must die. Adam and Eve, the guilty ones, were then covered with the "garments of skin." We see this more fully in chapter 4 when the offering of Abel was accepted, while Cain's was not. Opening up to us is the great plan of redemption that was perfectly fulfilled by Jesus Christ, the "Lamb of God." He willingly gave His life and suffered in our place. Then He clothes us in His righteousness.

Remember, the announcement God made to Satan that the woman's offspring "will crush your head" (Genesis 3:15), is the first news of a Redeemer. The enemy who had brought sin and death into the world will be conquered. When Christ was on the cross, Satan was only able to "strike his heel." At the same time, Satan's head, the center of his power, was crushed. Satan became a conquered foe. Christ will complete this victory "when he hands over the kingdom to God the Father" having "put all his enemies under his feet" (1 Corinthians 15:24,25).

NOTE: If you are completing this session in one meeting, ignore this break and continue with Step 3.

TWO-MEETING TRACK: If you want to spread this session over two meetings, **STOP** here and close in prayer. Inform group members of the content to be covered in your next meeting.

Begin your second meeting by asking questions to review the main ideas from the first half of the session.

What Bible chapters cover the first period of Bible history (Creation to the Call of Abraham)? (Genesis 1–11)

Who are the main characters of the first Period? (God, Adam, Eve, Noah)

What were the results of human disobedience? (Separation from God, entry of death and disorder into the world, murder, continual pursuit of evil)

What were the similarities between the sins of Adam and Eve, Cain, and the people of Babel? (Selfishness and pride—they all sought to satisfy their personal desires, and thought they knew what was best.)

What indications do we see in the first period of God's provision of a solution to the sin problem? (The prophecy of the woman's offspring crushing Satan pointing to Christ, the sacrificing of animals to clothe Adam and Eve and in Abel's offering, God's covenant with Noah)

Continue with Step 3 and conclude the session.

STEP 3 — ABRAHAM, ISAAC AND JACOB (*15 minutes*)

PERIOD 2/EVENT 1 — CALL OF ABRAHAM

Bible Time Line: page 3 (The Tower of Babel—Abraham Obeys God)

Present a brief background of the culture from which God called Abraham. Ask group members to raise their hands if they already knew that before God called Abraham out of Ur (around 2000 B.C.), the following were true:

- Egypt was strong and prosperous under the dynasties of the Old Kingdom and the pyramids of Gizeh (near modern Cairo) were already over 500 years old. And geometry was widely taught throughout the land.
- An astronomical observatory had been in use in Babylon for more than 150 years. Also, the Code of Hammurabi was about a century or two later.
- The Chinese Empire had been flourishing for centuries, and phonetic writing was in use there.
- Damascus was already a major city.

OPTION (*25 minutes*)
This option will add 10 minutes to the Step 3 section.

Assign each of the small groups one of the following New Testament passages to discover what they add to our knowledge of God's dealings with Abraham:

Acts 7:2-5	Romans 4:1-3
Romans 4:13-16	Galatians 3:6-9
Hebrews 6:12-15	Hebrews 11:8-10
James 2:21-24	

Allow the groups a few minutes to read and talk, then ask for volunteers to share the insights gained.

- Ur, named for the Babylonian moon god, was one of the oldest and most famous Babylonian cities.

Read aloud Genesis 12:1-8. Then point out these main features of God's call of Abraham:

- **God challenged Abraham to take action.**
- **God promised to bless Abraham, and to bless all humanity through him.**
- **God promised to make Abraham a great nation, and to give the land of Canaan to Abraham's descendants.**

Summarize this segment by inviting a volunteer to read aloud Genesis 15:1-6.

EVENTS 2 AND 3 — PREPARATION OF JACOB AND DESCENT INTO EGYPT

As time permits, invite volunteers to answer the following questions about Abraham's descendants:

- **How old were Abraham and Sarah when the son God had promised was born?** (Sarah was 90, Abraham was 100—Genesis 17:17-19)

Bible Time Line: page 4 (Isaac is Born—Isaac and Rebekah)

- **Who were the twin sons of Isaac and Rebekah?** (Esau and Jacob—Genesis 25:24-26)
- **How did "Jacob, the deceiver" become "Israel, who struggles with God"?** (Jacob, after years of deceiving his father, his brother and his uncle, wrestled with God the night before he returned to face Esau—Genesis 32:22-30.)
- **Who were the children of Jacob?** (Joseph, Benjamin, Judah, and nine other sons became the founders of the Twelve Tribes of Israel. Joseph's two sons, Manasseh and Ephraim, divided their father's inheritance. Levi, whose descendants were set apart for service to God did not receive a share of the land. Joseph also had one daughter, Dinah, who evidently had no children—Genesis 46:8-25.)
- **Which of Jacob's sons was instrumental in rescuing the family from starvation in a famine?** (Joseph—Genesis 45:4-7)
- **Where did God allow Jacob's family to dwell for over 400 years and grow into a strong nation?** (Goshen in Egypt—Genesis 46:31-34; Exodus 1:1-7)

Bible Time Line: pages 5-7 (Jacob and Joseph)

Summarize this study of Abraham's call and response: **Abraham was the greatest of the patriarchs; he was the beginning of the great nation, Israel, through whom we have received the Bible and the Messiah, the world's Redeemer. Abraham is the great example of saving faith, demonstrating his confidence in God's word by his obedient actions. There were times his faith faltered and his resulting actions created serious problems. Similarly, we also encounter times when belief comes hard.**

Invite two volunteers to read aloud 2 Peter 3:8,9 and Hebrews 10:23 as assurance of God's faithfulness in doing all that He has promised.

STEP 4 OPTION — JOSEPH *(15 minutes)*

In Step 3, the familiar story of Joseph was mentioned just briefly in getting a quick overview of the early history of Abraham's family. A closer look at Joseph's life is warranted, since the Bible spends more time telling it (Genesis 37; 39–50) than was given to the entire span of period 1.

Guide class members in a group retelling of the story of Joseph. Invite a volunteer to start the story. After a few sentences, ask for someone else to volunteer to pick up the narrative from that point. Continue this way until the story is completed, seeking to involve as many people as possible (without putting anyone on the spot). If the story gets off track or a major incident is skipped or told incorrectly, jump in with a comment or question (e.g., "Does anyone remember what had happened earlier so that Joseph was thought of to interpret the king's dream?").

Read aloud Acts 7:9-15, Stephen's summary of Joseph's life in his speech before the Sanhedrin (the Jewish council or tribunal, which governed most of the internal affairs of Palestine during the period of Roman rule). Then ask for a show of hands of those who prefer Stephen's version and those who like the one the class just offered.

GETTING PERSONAL *(5 minutes)*

Summarize the second period of Bible history (Call of Abraham to Coming out of Egypt):

The Greatest Fact: Birth of the Nation Israel (Genesis 12:1-7)
The Greatest Truth: Walking by Faith (Genesis 15:6)

Although Abraham is the great example of living by faith and risking all to obey God, we see the pattern continued in the lives of Isaac, Jacob and Joseph (Hebrews 11:20-22).

Encourage group members to consider these examples in light of the call we have all received, which Paul described in Romans 12:1,2: **"Therefore, I urge you, brothers, in view of God's mercy, to offer your bodies as living sacrifices, holy and pleasing to God—this is your spiritual act of worship. Do not conform any longer to the pattern of this world, but be transformed by the renewing your mind. Then you will be able to test and approve what God's will is—his good, pleasing and perfect will."**

Pray for one another about specific areas of your life that God will help you learn to live by faith and risk with Him to obey Him.

OPTION *(10 minutes)*

This option will add 5 minutes to the Getting Personal section.

Show the top of "The Periods of Bible History Outline" transparency as you lead the class in a quick review of the first two periods:

PERIOD	PEOPLE	EVENTS	SCRIPTURE
1. Creation to Call of Abraham	Adam & Eve Noah	1. Creation 2. Fall and Promise 3. Redemption 4. Flood 5. Judgment of Babel	Genesis 1–11
2. Call of Abraham to Coming out of Egypt	Abraham Isaac Jacob Joseph Job	1. Call of Abraham 2. Preparation of Jacob 3. Descent into Egypt	Genesis 12–50 Job 1–42

Assign class members to read the first two chapters in *What the Bible Is All About* or chapters 2 and 3 in the *Quick Reference Edition.* Encourage them to read the book of Genesis, especially the "Selected Bible Reading" suggestions at the end of chapter 2 in *What the Bible Is All About.*

Preview the next session by referring the class to the poem on pages 24-26 of *What the Bible Is All About.* If time permits, take a few minutes to lead the class in reciting the poem up through First and Second Samuel. Repeating the poem in each class session is an excellent device to help class members learn, not only the sequence of the books of the Bible, but a quick description of the contents of each book.

PERIOD OF GREAT DELIVERANCE

FORESHADOWING THE CROSS AND RESURRECTION

Coming out of Egypt to Coronation of Saul

S·E·S·S·I·O·N · K·E·Y·S

▌KEY VERSE

"The Lord is my strength and my song; he has become my salvation. He is my God, and I will praise him, my father's God, and I will exalt him." Exodus 15:2

▌KEY IDEA

God delivered Israel from bondage in Egypt to establish His people as a strong nation so that it might bless every nation through Christ.

▌KEY RESOURCES

- Exodus—1 Samuel 7
- Selected New Testament references
- Chapters 3-9 in *What the Bible Is All About* and/or chapters 3-10 in *What the Bible Is All About: Quick Reference Edition*

PREPARATION

Provide blank name tags and felt pens. Make a tag for yourself.

Display each of six Periods of Bible History posters made for Session 1.

Display pages 1-7 from *The Big Picture Bible Time Line*. Have ready pages 8-21.

Have ready copies of "The Six Mountain Peaks of Bible History" and "The Bible—A Library of Smaller Books" for each person who needs one. Have ready overhead transparencies of

the pages and "The Periods of Bible History Outline." Also have an overhead projector.

For Choice 1: Have ready sheets of blank paper and pencils (one of each for every two or three people in the class).

For Choice 2: Provide nine or more blank transparencies and at least the same number of transparency pens. (Or have large sheets of paper and felt markers.)

Prepare a basket or bowl with a simple "treat"—candy, nuts, etc.—at least one treat per person.

Have ready eight large sheets of newsprint or butcher paper plus a selection of felt pens.

CHRIST'S BLOODLINE

ABRAHAM   ISAAC   JACOB

SESSION 2 AT A GLANCE

SECTION	ONE SESSION PLAN		TWO SESSION PLAN	WHAT YOU'LL DO
Time Schedule	60 Minutes	More than 60 Minutes	60 Minutes (each session)	
Getting Started	10	10-20	*Session One:* 20	Focus on the Big Picture in Scripture
Getting into the Word	40	85	40	Learn Major Persons and Events of the Period
Step 1	10	20	20	Step 1—Exodus from Egypt
Step 2	10	20	20	Step 2—Giving of the Law
			Session Two Start Option: 10	
Step 3	10	15	**15**	Step 3—Wilderness Wanderings
Step 4	5	10	10	Step 4—Conquest of Canaan
Step 5	5	10	10	Step 5—Judges Rule the Land
Getting Personal	10	10-15	15	Apply Basic Truths to Your Life

S·E·S·S·I·O·N · P·L·A·N

LEADER'S CHOICE

Two-meeting Track: This session is designed to be completed in one 60-minute meeting. If you want to extend the session over two meetings and allow group members more time for discussion, **END** your first meeting and **BEGIN** your second meeting at the stop-and-go symbol in the session plan.

The boxes marked with the clock symbol provide optional learning experiences to extend this session over two meetings or to accommodate a session longer than 60-75 minutes.

GETTING STARTED (10 minutes)

CHOICE 1: SIX PERIODS OF BIBLE HISTORY

Welcome people as they arrive and guide them to complete and wear a name tag. Instruct them to find a partner or two and select one of the events shown on *Time Line* pages 1-7, which are displayed on the wall. Then, each pair or trio locates the Bible passage for that event and seeks to come up with one question about that event, which they can ask in order to "stump" the rest of the class. You may provide blank paper and pencils to aid in this process. Reserve 5 minutes for having group members ask the questions they wrote.

Invite volunteers to read aloud their questions. Lead the class in cheering for those who succeed in answering correctly—as well as for any groups that succeed in stumping the class. When time is up, pass around the treat you provided, explaining that it is for all those who answered a question, those who asked one no one else could answer, and those who need a little encouragement for not being able to do either one this time.

Point out that several hundred years pass between the last events of Genesis and the events of Exodus, and that the events from Exodus through 1 Samuel (the period being studied today) span almost 500 more years.

CHOICE 2: BOOKS OF THE BIBLE POEM

Welcome people as they arrive and guide them to complete and wear a name tag. Invite each person to find a partner or two, then assign each pair or trio one of the opening lines or phrases (at least up through Samuel) of the poem on page 24 of *What the Bible Is All About*.

Instruct people to work together to letter their line or phrase at the top of a transparency (or large piece of paper), then quickly add a word, symbol or simple sketch that fits their assigned book of the Bible. As groups begin finishing their transparencies, project them on the overhead (or mount sheets on the wall). When all groups are finished, lead the class in reciting the poem as you project the transparencies (or point to the sheets). Point out that several hundred years pass between the end of Genesis and the events of Exodus, and that the events from Exodus

through 1 Samuel (the period being studied today) span almost 300-500 more years.

If time allows, and if the class is enjoying learning this poem, slip a sheet of paper across the top of the overhead projector (or use other sheets of paper) to cover the words of the poem while showing the symbols or sketches. See how well the class does in reciting the poem using just those visual cues.

GETTING INTO THE WORD (40 minutes)

Step 1—Exodus from Egypt

Step 2—Giving of the Law

Step 3—Wilderness Wanderings

Step 4—Conquest of Canaan

Step 5—Judges Rule the Land

STEP 1—EXODUS FROM EGYPT
(15 minutes)

Divide the class into eight groups. Give each group a large sheet of newsprint or butcher paper and several felt markers. Instruct the groups that they will each be assigned a brief section of the first half of the book of Exodus. (*Exodus* is a Greek word meaning "way out.") Their task is to skim the section headings, looking for the major event or events of their chapters, then to quickly draw a road sign (e.g., a "Stop" sign, a "One Way" sign, etc.) that summarizes those events. Above or below their sign should be the chapter numbers and a very brief phrase about the chapter events. For example, if a similar assignment had been made for the last part of Genesis, a group assigned chapters 46 and 47 might have drawn a mileage sign: "Goshen 20 km—Genesis 46,47—Jacob Moves to Egypt."

Assign the groups the following chapters:

 GETTING STARTED OPTION: (20 minutes)
This option will add 10 minutes to the end of the Getting Started section.

Ask for volunteers to name significant characters or events between Coming out of Egypt and the Coronation of Saul. List these on the left side of the chalkboard or a blank transparency.

After several minutes, guide the class in sequencing these names and events in chronological order. Ask, **Which of these people/events came first?** Write the names on the right side of the chalkboard or transparency. If the class is not sure where a person or event fits in the sequence, circle that name or event in the original list and add a question mark.

When all names and events have either been placed in sequence or circled, start at the top of the list and invite volunteers to tell one significant thing they recall about that event or person.

Transition into today's study with this brief comment: **The period between the Coming out of Egypt and the Coronation of Saul can be thought of as the Period of Great Leaders. Although there were great leaders in other periods, this span of almost 300-500 years is the only extended time in history when Israel was led by people chosen by God, not by human decisions. These leaders were not perfect, nor was life in Israel idyllic, but God raised up men and women to deliver His people from oppression.**

Exodus 1,2
Exodus 3,4
Exodus 5,6
Exodus 7–10
Exodus 11,12
Exodus 13–15
Exodus 16–18
Exodus 19,20

Allow about 5 minutes for groups to work. Have them tape or tack their road signs to the wall, then invite a volunteer from each group to explain their sign in 30 seconds or less.

Summarize this overview: **The central event of the book of Exodus is clearly the Passover. This is true for the Christian fully as much as for the Jewish people. Henrietta Mears wrote: "Exodus 12 gives us the thrilling story of the Passover, the clearest Old Testament picture of our individual salvation through faith in the shed blood of our Lord Jesus Christ. In this chapter is the basis for calling Christ the *Lamb of God*, *Christ our Passover*, and the many tender references to His crucifixion as the death of our own Passover Lamb"** (*What the Bible Is All About*, pp. 45,46).

Read aloud 1 Peter 1:18-21 as an example of one passage about Christ that builds on our understanding of Christ as the Passover Lamb.

Bible Time Line: pages 9-10 (Moses)

STEP 2 — GIVING OF THE LAW (10 minutes)

Present an overview of the remaining chapters of Exodus in which the law was given to Israel at Mount Sinai:

Chapters 19–24: God gave Ten Commandments (written by God's hand on stone tablets—Exodus 24:12) and other laws dealing with social relationships and religious observances.

Chapters 25–31: God gave instructions for building the Tabernacle. Two distinct structures are mentioned in Exodus, and they are both called the "tent of meeting." Before the Tabernacle was built, there was a temporary structure to which people came when Moses was meeting with God (Exodus 33:7-11). This name was also applied to the Tabernacle, indicating that it was the place where God met with His people (29:42,43).

Chapter 32: The people sinned by building and worshiping a golden calf. While still high upon Mount Sinai, Moses heard the noise of their revelry and rushed down the mountain. In anger, Moses broke the stone tablets.

Chapters 33,34: Moses saw God's glory, then carved new stone tablets and wrote again the Ten Commandments (34:28).

Chapters 35–39: The Tabernacle and the Ark of the Covenant (or Testimony) were built.

Chapter 40: The Tabernacle was set up.

Bible Time Line: pages 11,12 (Ten Commandments—Ark of the Covenant)

Introduce the class to the book of Leviticus, named after the Levites. Levi was one of Jacob's twelve sons, and his descendants were specially chosen by God to be the priests, musicians and workers who served God at the Tabernacle. Henrietta Mears called Leviticus "God's picture book for the children of Israel to help them in their religious training. Every picture pointed forward to the work of Jesus Christ" (p. 51, *What the Bible Is All About*).

Chapters 1–7: The Offerings—These are detailed provisions for how unholy people may approach a holy God.

OPTION (*20 minutes*)
This option will add 10 minutes to the Step 1 section.

Point out that Bible scholars, historians and archaeologists have expended a great deal of effort attempting to identify the date of the Exodus and the identity of the pharaoh (king) at the time. Two main positions have been advanced, each with strong arguments in support. One view proposes that the "new king, who did not know about Joseph" (Exodus 1:8) was Ahmose I, the first Egyptian ruler after expelling the Hyksos who had ruled Egypt from 1700 to about 1570 B.C. Then Thutmose II would have been the ruler when the child Moses was brought into the palace under the protection of the Princess Hatshepsut. Thutmose III, who detested even the memory of Hatshepsut, is identified as the ruler at the time of the Exodus.

The other view proposes Seti I was the ruler who did not know about Joseph and Ramses II, nor his son Merneptah as the king at the time of the Exodus. Although each view has its advocates, settling the issue is not necessary to this study. However, it is significant that the extensive search for historical and archaeological evidence has uncovered significant cultural, political and military evidence of that period, which illuminates our understanding of Scripture.

Call on three group members who read well aloud, and assign them to read (with expression!) Exodus 3:1-6 in order to gain a sense of the deepening revelation of Himself, which God was giving to His people at this time. Have one person read the words and thoughts of Moses, another the words of God; have the third be the narrator and read all other text. When the reading is finished, ask, **What does this familiar incident reveal about God?**

Read aloud one or more other passages from this section of Exodus to share further glimpses into the revelation of God's character and purpose:
Exodus 3:13-15—authentic, consistent, absolute, self-evident
Exodus 4:10-12—Creator, Helper
Exodus 6:2-6—faithful, keeping His covenants
Exodus 15:26—healing
Exodus 20:4-6—both jealous and loving

Each sacrifice shows a dimension of Christ's ultimate provision of full atonement for sin.

Chapters 8–10: The Priests—These instructions describe how the priests were to represent the people before God. Similarly, Christ is our High Priest (Hebrews 2:17; 4:14).

Chapters 11–22: Daily Living—These regulations focus on food, health and interpersonal relationships. Christ came to bring fulness of health and life (John 10:10).

Chapter 16: The Day of Atonement—The great day of confession and forgiveness, the only day a priest could enter the Most Holy Place in the Tabernacle, offering sacrifice for all the sins of the Israelites. Christ came to make atonement (Romans 3:25), providing access for us into the very presence of God (Hebrews 4:16).

Chapters 23–25: The Feasts—Eight holidays or festivals were established for worship and refreshing. As with sacrifices, each feast reveals an important aspect of Christ's mission on our behalf.

Chapters 26–27: Rewards, Punishments and Promises—The book concludes with very practical guidelines for obedience and disobedience, plus instructions on how to fulfill special promises made to the Lord. Christ is the ultimate example of obedience and dedication to the Lord.

OPTION (*20 minutes*)
This option will add 10 minutes to the Step 2 section.

Ask the following questions in order to lead the group in exploring several issues related to the giving of the law. Encourage each person to locate and read each passage, then participate in responding to the question:

According to Exodus 19:5, what was God's purpose in giving His law to Israel?

According to Exodus 19:8, what was the initial reaction of the people to the idea that God would give them His laws?

According to Psalm 19:7-11, what is the value for people of God's law?

According to Galatians 3:19, what was the ultimate purpose of the law?

According to Galatians 3:22-25, what is the role of God's law in our lives?

NOTE: If you are completing this session in one meeting, ignore this break and continue with Step 3.

TWO-MEETING TRACK: If you want to spread this session over two meetings, **STOP** here and close in prayer. Inform group members of the content to be covered in your next meeting.

START OPTION (10 minutes) Begin your second meeting by asking questions such as these to review the main ideas from the first half of the session.

Where would you look in the Bible:

To read about God calling Moses to lead Israel out of slavery? (Exodus 3,4)

To find the crossing of the Red Sea? (Exodus 14)

To read the Ten Commandments? (Exodus 20)

To learn about the Day of Atonement? (Leviticus 16)

Invite volunteers to tell one insight they have gained (or been reminded of) about the Bible from their study thus far. Be prepared to share an example of your own learning to help people feel comfortable admitting something they needed to learn or remember.

Continue with Step 3 and conclude the session.

STEP 3 — WILDERNESS WANDERINGS
(*10 minutes*)

Point out that Israel spent a little over a year at Sinai, then God determined it was time to move on toward the land He had promised.

Divide the class into eight groups. Assign each group one of the following questions to research and answer:

1. Why did God instruct Moses to conduct a census? (Numbers 1:1-4; 26:1,2)
2. How did God guide Israel's movements in the desert? (Numbers 9:15-18; 10:11-13)
3. Why did the people complain? (Numbers 11:4-9)
4. What was God's plan to help Moses deal with the burdens of leadership? (Numbers 11:14-17)
5. Why didn't the Israelites go directly from Sinai into Canaan, the land God had promised? (Numbers 13:30–14:4)
6. What was Moses' greatest failure? (Numbers 20:2-12)
7. What symbolic act of Moses was referred to by Jesus in describing his bringing salvation to mankind? (Numbers 21:4-9; John 3:14,15)
8. Who did God choose to succeed Moses as leader of Israel? (Numbers 27:12-20)

Allow several minutes for groups to locate and read their passages, then invite a volunteer from each one to share their question and the answer they found.

Point out that the book of Deuteronomy (the "second law") is the record of three messages Moses delivered shortly before his death. These messages were to remind the people of all God had done for them and the laws God had given to guide their daily living. These truths were of vital importance as the nation ended 40 years in the desert and prepared to advance into the promised land of Canaan.

Bible Time Line: page 13 (God Leads the Israelites/Joshua and Caleb)

STEP 3 OPTION (*15 minutes*)
This option will add 5 minutes to the Step 3 section.

Lead the group in discovering some of the references in Deuteronomy that Jesus quoted. Assign the following verses to volunteers to read aloud. Ask the class to identify when Jesus used each verse and whether or not Jesus supported the idea or used it to introduce a new teaching:

Deuteronomy 8:3 (Matthew 4:4—His temptation)
Deuteronomy 6:16 (Matthew 4:7—His temptation)
Deuteronomy 6:13 (Matthew 4:10—His temptation)
Deuteronomy 6:5 (Matthew 22:37—when asked by a Pharisee to tell what is the greatest commandment)
Deuteronomy 5:16-20 (Luke 18:20—talking with rich ruler)
Deuteronomy 19:15 (Matthew 18:16—talking about correcting a brother who sins against you)
Deuteronomy 19:21; 24:1 (Matthew 5:31,38—talking about fulfillment of various laws, Jesus offered significant new insights)

Summarize the findings from this activity: **Jesus quoted many Old Testament books, Deuteronomy among them. Usually He affirmed the original instruction. Occasionally He introduced totally new concepts, following a quote with the phrase, "But I tell you." In so doing, Jesus not only honored the validity of Deuteronomy and the other sacred writings, He used them to open people's thinking to truths they had never seen before.**

STEP 4 — CONQUEST OF CANAAN
(5 minutes)

The book of Joshua shows God's leader, Joshua, bringing God's people into the Promised Land. (The name Joshua means "the Lord is salvation.") In the New Testament we see another leader of the same name (*Jesus* is the Greek form of the same name) who came to take God's people into the promised land of eternal life in God's presence.

Provide a brief overview of the Conquest as recorded in the book of Joshua:

Chapters 1–4: Entering the Land—Joshua, by now an elderly man, led the people in a miraculous crossing of the Jordan River.

Chapters 5–12: Conquering the Land—Jericho was overrun by God's power, leading to a series of battles against the inhabitants of Canaan, reestablishing God's claim as He had promised Abraham. After many victories, mixed with some defeats, against the idolatrous and immoral Canaanites, "Joshua took the entire land, just as the Lord had directed Moses" (Joshua 11:23).

Chapters 13–22: Dividing the Land—Joshua divided the conquered land among the tribes of Israel. Remember, the Levites, having been set apart for service to God, did not receive a portion of land. The offerings of all the other tribes were to support the Levites. Also note, the half tribes of

Manasseh and Ephraim were the descendants of Joseph's two sons (Joshua 14:4).

Chapters 23,24: Joshua's Farewell and Death—Joshua died at the age of 110 (Joshua 24:29) having seen the Lord's salvation in the land of his inheritance.

OPTION (*10 minutes*)
This option will add 5 minutes to the Step 4 section.

Bible Time Line: pages 14-17 (Rahab—Joshua)

Lead the group in considering two of the most intriguing characters in the book of Joshua: Rahab and Caleb.

Rahab: A prostitute who hid two of Israel's spies because of her faith that "the Lord has given this land to you" (Joshua 2:8). In return for her faith and bravery, Rahab and her family were spared the destruction that visited Jericho. In addition, her grandson was Boaz, the husband of Ruth and great grandfather of David—and thus she was an ancestor of Jesus (Joshua 2; 6:17-25; Matthew 1:5; Hebrews 11:31; James 2:25).

Caleb and Joshua were the only spies sent by Moses who believed God would give Israel victory in the Promised Land (Numbers 13,14). These two were the only adults in Israel who survived the 40 years in the wilderness and actually entered the Promised Land (Numbers 26:65). After most of the land had been conquered, Caleb was given Hebron as his inheritance (Joshua 14:6-14). His daughter was given in marriage to Othniel (Joshua 15:13-17; Judges 1:12,13), who later became the first of the judges of Israel (Judges 3:7-11).

STEP 5 — JUDGES RULE THE LAND
(5 minutes)

Introduce the story of the judges:

The book of Judges covers about 350 years in Israel's history, a period when "Israel had no king; everyone did as he saw fit" (Judges 17:6; 21:25). God raised up leaders called judges to rescue the nation from the consequences of their sin. This era is one of repeated cycles of sin, oppression and deliverance. Israel's sin resulted in oppression at the hands of nations that had been allowed to remain in the land and whose heathen practices corrupted the morals and worship of Israel. When the people finally realized their need of God, God sent a deliverer. Accounts of 12 judges (8 of whom are mentioned only very briefly) are given in the book of Judges, with the stories of Eli and Samuel, who was the last and greatest of them all, told in the book of 1 Samuel. (The incidents told in the book of Ruth occurred sometime during the era of the judges.)

List on the chalkboard or overhead the names of the six most famous judges, where their stories are, and their main accomplishments:

- Othniel—Judges 3—Defeated Aram
- Deborah—Judges 4,5—Defeated Canaan
- Gideon—Judges 6–8—Tore down altar to Baal, defeated Midian
- Jephthah—Judges 10–12—Defeated Ammon
- Samson—Judges 13–16—Defeated Philistia
- Samuel—1 Samuel 1–25:1—Defeated Philistia, anointed Saul and David

As a final act of rejecting God's authority, the people demanded a king. Rather than obeying God's laws and following His leaders, they continued even further down the path of rebellion.

Bible Time Line: pages 18-21 (Israel Worships Idols—Samuel)

OPTION (*10 minutes*)
This option will add 5 minutes to the Step 5 section.
    Return the class to small groups. Instruct each group to choose one of the judges listed on the board or overhead. They are to locate and quickly skim the story of that judge. Call time after several minutes and ask everyone to turn to a partner and share one significant fact about that judge.

GETTING PERSONAL (*10 minutes*)

Summarize the third period of Bible history (Coming out of Egypt to Coronation of Saul):

The Greatest Fact: The Giving of God's Law (Exodus 20)
The Greatest Truth: The Passover (Exodus 12)

A perfect lamb was taken on the passover night and its blood was sprinkled on the doorposts of the house. Upon seeing this marking, the angel of death passed over—spared—that house. So Christ, the Lamb of God, spilled His blood for us. He was without blemish, perfect in holiness (1 Peter 1:19). By receiving Christ into our hearts as our Savior, we receive life instead of death. "And this is the testimony: God has given us eternal life, and this life is in his Son. He who has the Son has life; he who does not have the Son of God does not have life" (1 John 5:11,12).

Guide class members in considering several other New Testament statements about Christ bringing life in place of death:

Romans 6:22,23
Hebrews 2:9
Hebrews 9:22,28
1 Peter 2:24

Offer to meet and pray individually with anyone interested in talking about receiving the life that Christ offers. Pray in pairs for any personal needs and thank God for the life He has given you through Christ living in you.

OPTION (*15 minutes*)
This option will add 5 minutes to the Getting Personal section.
Show the top of "The Periods of Bible History Outline" transparency as you lead the class in a quick review of the first three periods:

PERIOD	PEOPLE	EVENTS	SCRIPTURE
1. Creation to Call of Abraham	Adam & Eve Noah	1. Creation 2. Fall and Promise 3. Redemption 4. Flood 5. Judgment of Babel	Genesis 1–11
2. Call of Abraham to Coming out of Egypt	Abraham Isaac Jacob Joseph Job	1. Call of Abraham 2. Preparation of Jacob 3. Descent into Egypt	Genesis 12–50 Job 1–42
3. Coming out of Egypt to Coronation of Saul	Moses Joshua The Judges: Deborah Gideon Samson Samuel	1. Exodus from Egypt 2. Giving of the Law 3. Wilderness Wanderings 4. Conquest of Canaan 5. Judges Rule the Land	Exodus 1–18 Exodus 19–Leviticus Numbers–Deuteronomy Joshua Judges–1 Samuel 7

Assign class members to read chapters 3-9 in *What the Bible Is All About* or chapters 3-10 in the *Quick Reference Edition*. Encourage them to read the book of Exodus, especially the "Selected Bible Reading" suggestions at the end of chapter 3 in *What the Bible Is All About*.

Preview the next session by referring the class to the poem on pages 24-26 of *What the Bible Is All About*. If time permits, take a few minutes to lead the class in reciting the poem up through First and Second Chronicles. Repeating the poem in each class session is an excellent device to help class members learn, not only the sequence of the books of the Bible, but a quick description of the contents of each book.

PERIOD OF KINGS

FORESHADOWING THE KINGDOM RULE OF CHRIST

Coronation of Saul to Captivity in Babylon

S·E·S·S·I·O·N · K·E·Y·S

▌KEY VERSE

"Righteousness exalts a nation, but sin is a disgrace to any people." Proverbs 14:34

▌KEY IDEA

Israel rejected God's leadership and was ultimately destroyed by the sinful practices of her kings and people.

▌KEY RESOURCES

■ Selected New Testament references

■ Chapters 9-11,16-19,22-24 in *What the Bible Is All About* and/or chapters 10-15,20-27,30-38 in *What the Bible Is All About: Quick Reference Edition*

PREPARATION

If class members are still getting to know each other, continue to provide blank name tags and felt pens. Make a tag for yourself.

Display each of six Period of Bible History posters made for Session 1.

Display pages 1-21 from *The Big Picture Bible Time Line*. Have ready pages 22-41.

Have ready copies of "The Six Mountain Peaks of Bible History" and "The Bible—A Library of Smaller Books" for each

person who needs one. Also have ready overhead transparencies of these pages plus "The Periods of Bible History Outline" and "Kings and Prophets." Have an overhead projector set up.

For Choice 1: On large index cards, letter the names of an equal number of kings and prophets of Israel and Judah so that you have one card for each person in the class. If your class is small, select the more familiar characters. Use colored markers to designate in which of these categories each name fits:

Red = Kings of Combined Nation (Saul, David, Solomon)

Orange = Kings of Northern Kingdom (Israel—Jereboam-Hoshea)

Black = Kings of Southern Kingdom (Judah—Rehoboam-Zedekiah)

Green = Major Prophets* (Samuel, Elijah, Elisha, Isaiah, Jeremiah)

Blue = Minor Prophets* (Hosea-Zephaniah)

Provide pins or masking tape for people to use in attaching these cards to their clothing.

*NOTES ON THESE PROPHETS: Samuel, Elijah and Elisha are listed as Major Prophets because of their importance, but they are not typically listed as "Major Prophets" as they did not write prophetic books. This activity will not include prophets who ministered mainly after the fall of Jerusalem (Daniel, Ezekiel, Zechariah, Haggai, Malachi).

For Step 2 Option, letter on 10 index cards each of the following references from prophetic messages:
1 Kings 21:20-22

2 Kings 6:21-23
Isaiah 1:15-18
Jeremiah 3:11-15
Hosea 1:1-5
Joel 2:21-24
Amos 9:11-15
Micah 5:1-4
Habakkuk 2:18-20
Zephaniah 3:14-17

For Step 3, prepare a chart or overhead transparency listing the key dates and references of the fall of Israel and Judah:
Fall of Israel to Assyria—722 B.C. (2 Kings 17:1-15)
Judah's first deportation to Babylon—605 B.C. (2 Kings 24:1-4; Daniel 1:1-3)
Judah's second deportation to Babylon—597 B.C. (2 Kings 24:8-14; Ezekiel 1:1-3)
Destruction of Jerusalem—586 B.C. (2 Kings 25:1-12)

CHRIST'S BLOODLINE

JUDAH   DAVID

SESSION 3 AT A GLANCE

SECTION	ONE SESSION PLAN		TWO SESSION PLAN	WHAT YOU'LL DO
Time Schedule	60 Minutes	More than 60 Minutes	60 Minutes (each session)	
Getting Started	10	10-20	*Session One:* 20	Focus on the Big Picture in Scripture
Getting into the Word	40	75	40	Learn Major Persons and Events of the Period
Step 1	15	20	20	Step 1—Kingdom United
Step 2	15	20	20	Step 2—Kingdom Divided
			Session Two Start Option: 10	
Step 3	10	35	35	Step 3—Downfall of the Kingdom
Getting Personal	10	10-15	15	Apply Basic Truths to Your Life

S·E·S·S·I·O·N · P·L·A·N

LEADER'S CHOICE

Two-meeting Track: This session is designed to be completed in one 60-minute meeting. If you want to extend the session over two meetings and allow group members more time for discussion, **END** your first meeting and **BEGIN** your second meeting at the stop-and-go symbol in the session plan.

The boxes marked with the clock symbol provide optional learning experiences to extend this session over two meetings or to accommodate a session longer than 60-75 minutes.

GETTING STARTED *(10 minutes)*

CHOICE 1: KINGS AND PROPHETS (A PREVIEW)

Welcome people as they arrive; have each person select and wear an index card with the name of a king or prophet. Instruct people to mingle through the room, looking for other kings or prophets their character may have known. Encourage them to ask questions such as, "Hello, Saul. My name is Amos. Do you know anything about me?" When someone finds a contemporary of his or her character, they should stay together and seek to find anyone else who may have known them. Invite group members to look in their Bibles for information they can discover.

After people mingle and talk, ask everyone to arrange themselves in "rough" chronological order across the back of the room: Far left = 1040 B.C. (Coronation of Saul); Center = 800 B.C. (Jehoash becomes king in Israel, Joash is king in Judah, and Elisha and Joel are prophets); Far right = 585 B.C. (Captivity/Fall of Jerusalem). Those who do not know where their character fits come to the front.

When everyone is situated, introduce today's study: **Obviously, some characters are more familiar than others and are easier to place. Besides, if we all knew everything about all these characters, we could perhaps skip this group. However, our goal is not just to learn which king knew which prophet, but to discover the significance of nearly 500 years in the history of God's dealings with His people.**

CHOICE 2: SIX PERIODS OF BIBLE HISTORY (A REVIEW)

Welcome people as they arrive. Instruct people to find a partner or two. Give each pair or trio two blank sheets of paper and two felt pens. They are to choose one character from the *Time Line*

pages on the wall, then letter that name vertically on one sheet of paper. They place the second sheet next to the first one. On the second sheet, in line with the letters of the name, they write words that begin with each letter of the name and that describe something about that person. In lettering the words, do not repeat the initial letter.

As each acrostic is completed, collect the second sheet from each group. Hold them up, one at a time, and let the class guess the character by figuring out the missing initial letters. For example:

A - lone
D - eceived
A - nimals
M - an

When all characters have been named, introduce today's study:

Obviously, some characters are more familiar than others and are easier to describe. Besides, if we knew everything about all these characters, we could perhaps skip this group. As we move into the next period of Bible history, the Coronation of Saul to Captivity in Babylon, our goal is not just to learn facts, but to discover the significance of nearly 500 years in the history of God's dealings with His people.

GETTING STARTED OPTION: *(20 minutes)*
This option will add 10 minutes to the end of the Getting Started section.

Divide into groups of four. Starting with the person in each group who will have the next birthday, each person tells one thing they feel they have gained from this study thus far. Encourage people to think beyond the acquisition of interesting information, and to consider what implications this knowledge has for their lives. Each person tells their story in one minute or less.

Ask for volunteers to share with the class one interesting or significant benefit that was shared in their group.

GETTING INTO THE WORD (40 minutes)

Step 1—Kingdom United

Step 2—Kingdom Divided

Step 3—Downfall of the Kingdom

STEP 1 — KINGDOM UNITED (15 minutes)

Remind the class that for about 500 years—since the conquest of Canaan—God had ruled Israel through judges He selected. These judges were raised up each time the people rejected God and brought disaster upon themselves. However, the people never learned that their pattern of willful rebellion was the cause of their troubles.

Ask class members to answer the following questions, looking up the references given.

In 1 Samuel 8:5, what solution did they demand in an attempt to strengthen the nation against enemy attacks? (They wanted a king.)

According to 1 Samuel 8:6-9, what was God's response to this demand? (He allowed them to have their way, but instructed Samuel to warn them of the consequences of this action.)

What were some of the attributes of Saul that qualified him to be king? 1 Samuel 9:1,15–17,21; 10:9,15,16,20–24 (He was physically impressive, chosen by God, humble, and God changed his heart.)

As told in 1 Samuel 13:11-14, and 15:17-23, what was Saul's great failure? (He disregarded God's commands.)

According to 1 Samuel 16:11-13, who did God choose to replace Saul? (David, the youngest son of Jesse)

Point out that 15 years passed from the time David was anointed (1025 B.C.) until the death of Saul and David was crowned king of Judah (1010 B.C.)—and another 7 years passed before David ruled all of Israel (1003 B.C.). Chapters 17–31 of 1 Samuel recount the decline of Saul as a leader as he repeatedly tried to kill David.

According to 2 Samuel 11, what was David's great sin? (He committed adultery with Bathsheba, then plotted the murder of her husband Uriah, one of his royal guard.)

What does Psalm 51:1,2 reveal about David, and why he was not rejected for his sins as Saul had been? (Instead of seeking to justify his actions, David confessed his sin and sought forgiveness.)

After David's sin, what does 2 Samuel 13:19-22,28,29 and 15:13,14 show as some of the results of David's sin? (The same sins David committed, lust and murder, were repeated within his own house.)

According to 1 Kings 1:32-35, who was chosen to follow David as king? (Solomon, who was David's son by Bathsheba)

In 1 Kings 3:5-9, what request did young Solomon ask of God? ("A discerning heart to govern...and to distinguish between right and wrong")

According to 1 Kings 6:1, what was Solomon's most obvious achievement? (Building the Temple)

How does 1 Kings 10:23-25 describe Solomon's wealth and wisdom? (Greater "than all the other kings of the earth")

According to 1 Kings 11:1-6, what was Solomon's great failure? (He married heathen women who "turned his heart after other gods.")

What does 1 Kings 11:11-13 reveal of God's response to Solomon's sin? (God predicted that the kingdom would be split, with Solomon's son retaining leadership of only one tribe. Only because of God's promises to David was the kingdom not stripped from Solomon.)

Bible Time Line: pages 22-30 (Philistines—Queen of Sheba)

> **OPTION** (20 minutes)
> This option will add 5 minutes to the Step 1 section.
> Divide the room into three sections. Assign to each section two passages that reveal insights about David and Solomon. Although it is impossible to be certain about the authorship of all parts of these books, there is much reason to respect the traditional view that credits David for many of the Psalms, and Solomon for much of Proverbs plus Ecclesiastes and Song of Songs.
>
> Section 1: Psalm 23 and 51
> Section 2: Proverbs 2:1-11 and 3:1-12
> Section 3: Ecclesiastes 12:8-14 and Song of Songs 1:9–2:1
> The poetic books will be looked at more thoroughly in the Step 3 Option later in this session.

STEP 2 — KINGDOM DIVIDED (15 minutes)

Select five good readers and assign each of them one of the following parts to read aloud from 1 Kings 12:1-16:

Narrator (reads all parts not in quotes)
Rehoboam (vv. 5,6,9,12,14)
Jeroboam and the whole assembly of Israel (vv. 4,16)
The Elders (v. 7)
The Young Men (vv. 10,11)

Instruct the rest of the class to follow along, looking for insights into the question, **What caused the division in the kingdom of Israel?**

When the readers finish, read aloud verse 20. Then invite the class to explain the reasons for the division. (Continuing tribal divisions between the north and south, animosity against the house of David [south] by those whose families had been loyal to Saul [north], God's judgment on Solomon for his involvement with foreign wives and their gods [1 Kings 11:9-13], God's promise to Jeroboam [1 Kings 11:28-32].)

Briefly summarize the history of the two kingdoms:

ISRAEL—THE NORTHERN KINGDOM

Israel had many advantages over Judah. Ten of the twelve tribes belonged to it. It outnumbered Judah three to one in population. They had greater military power and their land was more fertile. However, Jeroboam was afraid to let his people go to Jerusalem to worship, so he set up two golden calves for the people to worship at altars at Bethel and Dan. Even though idolatry was in disobedience to God's law, it had long been practiced in Israel, and merely continued a pattern set by Solomon.

Israel's spiritual condition became worse from that day. Judgment was pronounced on Jeroboam and his house, and the kings who followed him were noted for "walking in the ways of Jeroboam and in his sin, which he had caused Israel to commit" (1 Kings 15:34; see also 15:26 and 16:19).

Israel was warned often that unless they turned back to God and forsook their evil ways they would be destroyed. God sent prophets to warn them, such as Elijah, Elisha, Amos and Hosea, but the people and their leaders would not return to God. Frequent military coups led to a confusing succession of kings. Of the 19 kings, not one was a good man. Therefore, in 722 B.C. Assyria captured Samaria and carried Israel into captivity. (See 2 Kings 17.)

JUDAH — THE SOUTHERN KINGDOM

Although the Southern Kingdom did not have the resources of the Northern Kingdom, it was a much more stable nation than was Israel. The people were more united, with the tribe of Judah dominating its smaller neighbor, Simeon (Joshua 19:9). Also, the people and leaders were more faithful to God, perhaps because of having the Temple in the capital city of Jerusalem. Still, a minority of the twenty descendants of David who sat on the throne of Judah were comparatively good men (Asa, Jehoshaphat, Amaziah, Azariah, Uzziah, Jotham and Hezekiah, Josiah). Because of the periodic revivals of spiritual fidelity, the Kingdom of Judah received God's protection and endured longer than Israel. Over the centuries, God sent prophets such as Isaiah, Jeremiah, Joel, Micah, Habakkuk and Zephaniah to preach to the people of Judah.

Bible Time Line: pages 31-39 (Kingdom Divided—King Josiah)

OPTION (20 minutes)
This option will add 5 minutes to the Step 2 section.

Distribute the 10 index cards on which you have lettered references for prophetic messages. As the people who received the cards look up the references, explain that many of the messages of God's prophets were directed to specific, immediate situations. Others dealt obviously with events far in the future. Still others did both, using the current event to illustrate something of even greater importance that would happen much later. Some scholars disagree on some messages regarding what interpretation we should make.

As soon as the references have been located, invite those people to read aloud the message. After all have been read, remind people that these are just brief excerpts from many messages recorded in Scripture that were delivered during the centuries of the divided kingdom. (The prophetic books written during this period will be explored more fully in the Step 3 Option later in this session.)

NOTE: If you are completing this session in one meeting, ignore this break and continue with Step 3.

TWO-MEETING TRACK: If you want to spread this session over two meetings, **STOP** here and close in prayer. Inform group members of the content to be covered in your next meeting.

START OPTION (10 minutes) Begin your second meeting by inviting group members to form pairs or trios and share with each other one biblical incident studied thus far that has been significant to them. Be prepared to share an example of your own learning to help people feel comfortable talking. After several minutes of interaction, invite volunteers to share with the entire class one incident that was discussed in their smaller group.

Then continue with Step 3 and conclude the session.

STEP 3 — DOWNFALL OF THE KINGDOM *(10 minutes)*

Have people remain with the same pairs or trios. Divide the class into four sections. Show the chart or overhead transparency you prepared of the fall of Israel and Judah listing the dates of the following events:

Assign one section to read about the fall of Israel to Assyria in 722 B.C. (2 Kings 17:1-15).

Assign another section to read about the first deportation to Babylon of the leaders of Judah in 605 B.C. (2 Kings 24:1-4; Daniel 1:1-3).

Assign the third section to read about Judah's second deportation to Babylon in 597 B.C. (2 Kings 24:8-14; Ezekiel 1:1-3).

Assign the fourth section to read about the final destruction of Jerusalem and the end of the Kingdom of Judah in 586 B.C. (2 Kings 25:1-12).

Allow time for the groups to read their passages, then invite a volunteer from each section to tell in 25 words or less what happened in the section they read.

Ask, **What caused the downfall of Israel and Judah?** (Their continued idolatry and rebellion against God's commands in spite of repeated warnings delivered by God's prophets.)

Ask, **Why was Judah allowed to continue for more than 100 years after Israel's destruction?** (Because of God's promises to David and the godly leadership of some kings such as Hezekiah.)

Bible Time Line: pages 40-41 (Daniel Taken Captive—Fall of Jerusalem)

OPTION (*35 minutes*)
This option will add 25 minutes to the Step 3 section.

THE BOOKS OF POETRY (*10 minutes*)

Present a brief overview of the five poetic books whose writing and final compilation spans the time of the patriarchs (Job and Psalm 90) to after the return from Exile.

Job may be the oldest book of the Bible, and deals with one of the oldest problems: Why do good people suffer? Although the lengthy disputes between Job and his three friends focus on trying to understand the disasters that came upon Job, the introduction and conclusion, plus God's response that begins in chapter 38, give us a glimpse of God's sovereign purposes, which are far beyond human experience and understanding. Through the struggle to understand, Job moved from a theoretical understanding to a deeply personal relationship with God: "My ears had heard of you but now my eyes have seen you" (Job 42:5).

Psalms: This collection of 150 prayers and songs is located at the midpoint of the Bible. Collecting the psalms took place over many centuries and was probably completed no later than the third century B.C. By the time of Christ, it was the prayer book used in the Temple and the synagogues. As such, it is widely quoted in the New Testament, with at least twenty of these referring to Christ and His death.

Proverbs is a collection of wise sayings that have proven of great value in helping people decide what is the best thing to do in difficult situations. Solomon is credited as having written or collected most of these proverbs, with others being mentioned for contributing sections or working on the final selections (Proverbs 25:1; 30:1; 31:1).

Ecclesiastes: Solomon is also widely credited as being the author of this intense book in which all human pursuits are shown to be "meaningless, a chasing after the wind" (1:14; 2:11,17,26, and so on). The only reasonable response to this awareness is to love and obey God (12:9-14).

Song of Songs: (Also "Song of Solomon") The book is a beautiful love poem between husband (Solomon) and wife ("O Shulammite"—6:13). Many see in it a picture of the love between God and His people. The idea of God's people as a bride is expressed often in the prophetic books and is used by Paul in Ephesians 5 in describing the relationship between Christ and the Church.

After presenting this overview of the poetic books, lead the class in exploring some of the references to Christ found in the Psalms. While many psalms refer to the coming Messiah (e.g., Psalm 2; 16; 24; 40; 45; 68; 69; 72; 97; 110; 118), Psalm 22 gives a vivid picture of Jesus' death on Calvary. Divide the class into two sections. Have those in the first section locate and read aloud a psalm, with those in the other section reading aloud the companion New Testament reference:

Psalm 22:1	Matthew 27:46
Psalm 22:6,7	Luke 23:35,36
Psalm 22:12,13	Matthew 27:36,44
Psalm 22:16	John 19:34; 20:20
Psalm 22:18	John 19:23,24
Psalm 22:28	1 Corinthians 15:23,24

THE BOOKS OF PROPHECY (*15 minutes*)

Show the "Kings and Prophets" overhead transparency. Point out these facts about prophets:

There were many other prophets besides these (e.g., Nathan—2 Samuel 12:1).

There were women who declared God's messages (e.g., Huldah—2 Kings 22:14-20).

The time of the pre-exilic prophets, from Samuel (the first prophet) to Jeremiah, the period covered by the books of Samuel, Kings and Chronicles, was a period of about 500 years.

Most prophetic messages were delivered to Israel and/or Judah, however, some were also aimed at other nations. Several books are aimed exclusively at other peoples: Obadiah preached against Edom for helping Babylon defeat Judah; Nahum predicted the downfall of Nineveh, capital of Assyria; Jonah preached in Nineveh (although the real message of the book is aimed at those in Israel who felt superior to the heathen in Assyria).

Elijah, Elisha, Amos and Hosea delivered God's messages to Israel.

Joel, Isaiah, Micah, Jeremiah, Habakkuk and Zephaniah spoke to Judah.

The message of these prophets was amazingly consistent. Lead the class in locating and reading these passages that represent these main themes that recur throughout the prophetic books:

1. Hosea 7:8-16—God's people must turn from their sin. (Prophets were not sent when the people were obeying God.)
2. Jeremiah 9:13-16—God's people will be scattered among the nations. (This occurred with the captivity of Israel and Judah, and continues to this day.)
3. Isaiah 7:14; 9:6,7; 53:3-6—God will send a deliverer—His Chosen One. (Messiah)
4. Jeremiah 25:11,12; Micah 7:8-12—The Jews will return to their own land. (This began with the restoration of Judah after 70 years, and has remarkably been resumed during this century.)
5. Jeremiah 23:5,6; Micah 5:4—The Messiah will rule over the whole earth. (This glorious future vision is still to be completed.)

Conclude this summary of the prophetic messages by reading aloud what Jesus said to two of His followers on the day of His resurrection (Luke 24:25-27).

GETTING PERSONAL *(10 minutes)*

Summarize the fourth period of Bible history (Coronation of Saul to Captivity in Babylon):

The Greatest Fact: The Rise and Fall of the Kingdom
The Greatest Truth: Disobedience Brings Ruin

This most interesting period in the whole history of Israel is filled with great lessons and warnings. The principal one, which will be eternally true, is that righteousness is the basis upon which any person or nation rises or falls. How different the history of the world would have been if people and nations had heeded this warning and followed this precept (Proverbs 14:34).

Although we may not be able to control nations, we still must apply the lesson to our own lives. Let us not fall, like Solomon or Jeroboam, or like the nations of Israel and Judah, into the same trap that made their histories end in sorrow and defeat. Only as our lives are hid with Christ in God is true success, as God counts it, possible.

Lead the class in a period of silent prayer, encouraging each person to reflect on areas in their lives about which they need to confess and ask God's forgiveness.

Conclude this time of prayer by reading aloud God's promise of pardon and blessing from Isaiah 55:6-13 or Isaiah 43:25.

OPTION *(15 minutes)*
This option will add 5 minutes to the Getting Personal section.

Show the top of "The Periods of Bible History Outline" transparency as you lead the class in a quick review of the first four periods:

PERIOD	PEOPLE	EVENTS	SCRIPTURE
1. Creation to Call of Abraham	Adam & Eve Noah	1. Creation 2. Fall and Promise 3. Redemption 4. Flood 5. Judgment of Babel	Genesis 1–11
2. Call of Abraham to Coming out of Egypt	Abraham Isaac Jacob Joseph Job	1. Call of Abraham 2. Preparation of Jacob 3. Descent into Egypt	Genesis 12–50 Job 1–42
3. Coming out of Egypt to Coronation of Saul	Moses Joshua The Judges: Deborah Gideon Samson Samuel	1. Exodus from Egypt 2. Giving of the Law 3. Wilderness Wanderings 4. Conquest of Canaan 5. Judges Rule the Land	Exodus 1–18 Exodus 19–Leviticus Numbers–Deuteronomy Joshua Judges–1 Samuel 7
4. Coronation of Saul to Captivity in Babylon	Saul David Solomon Rehoboam Jeroboam Hezekiah Isaiah Jeremiah	1. Kingdom United 2. Kingdom Divided 3. Downfall of the Kingdom	1–2 Samuel 1 Kings 1–11 1 Chronicles 2 Chronicles 1–9 1 Kings 12–2 Kings 23 2 Chronicles 10–35 2 Kings 24, 25 2 Chronicles 36

Assign class members to read chapters 9-11 in *What the Bible Is All About* or 10-15 in the *Quick Reference Edition*. Encourage them to read the book of Psalms, especially the "Selected Bible Reading" suggestions at the end of chapter 16 in *What the Bible Is All About*.

Preview the next session by referring the class to the poem on pages 24-26 of *What the Bible Is All About*. If time permits, take a few minutes to lead the class in reciting the poem up through the Poetical Books section. Repeating the poem in each class session is an excellent device to help class members learn, not only the sequence of the books of the Bible, but a quick description of the contents of each book.

Period of Foreign Rulers

LOOKING FOR THE COMING MESSIAH

Captivity in Babylon to Christ

S·E·S·S·I·O·N · K·E·Y·S

▌KEY VERSE

"The Lord will be king over the whole earth. On that day there will be one Lord, and his name the only name." Zechariah 14:9

▌KEY IDEA

God's authority is not threatened by human neglect or rebellion; He will fulfill His promises.

▌KEY RESOURCES

■ Chapters 12-14,20,21,25 in *What the Bible Is All About* and/or chapters 16-18,28,29,39-42 in *What the Bible Is All About: Quick Reference Edition*

PREPARATION

Provide blank name tags and felt pens. Make a tag for yourself.

Display each of six Period of Bible History posters made for Session 1.

In chronological order, display pages 1-41 from *The Big Picture Bible Time Line*. Have ready pages 42-49.

Have ready copies of "The Six Mountain Peaks of Bible History" and "The Bible—A Library of Smaller Books" for each person who needs one. Also have ready overhead transparen-

cies of these pages plus "The Periods of Bible History Outline" and the "Kings and Prophets" chart to show on an overhead projector.

For Choice 1 provide four blank index cards for each person.

For Choice 2 provide a Post-it Note for each person.

For Getting Started Option write up to 10 questions about characters studied thus far. Follow the format of the questions in the "Survey Quiz" on page 161 of *What the Bible Is All About*.

CHRIST'S BLOODLINE

DAVID   CHRIST'S BIRTH

SESSION 4 AT A GLANCE

SECTION	ONE SESSION PLAN		TWO SESSION PLAN	WHAT YOU'LL DO
Time Schedule	60 Minutes	More than 60 Minutes	60 Minutes (each session)	
Getting Started	10	10-20	*Session One:* **20**	Focus on the Big Picture in Scripture
Getting into the Word	40	75	40	Learn Major Persons and Events of the Period
Step 1	15	20	20	Step 1—Captivity Under Babylon
Step 2	15	20	20	Step 2—Restoration Under Persia
			Session Two Start Option: **10**	
Step 3	10	35	35	Step 3—The Inter-testamental Period
Getting Personal	10	10-15	15	Apply Basic Truths to Your Life

S·E·S·S·I·O·N · P·L·A·N

LEADER'S CHOICE

Two-meeting Track: This session is designed to be completed in one 60-minute meeting. If you want to extend the session over two meetings and allow group members more time for discussion, **END** your first meeting and **BEGIN** your second meeting at the stop-and-go symbol in the session plan.

The boxes marked with the clock symbol provide optional learning experiences to extend this session over two meetings or to accommodate a session longer than 60-75 minutes.

GETTING STARTED (10 minutes)

CHOICE 1: KINGS AND PROPHETS

Welcome people as they arrive. Give each person four index cards. On each card they write the name of a different king or prophet studied thus far. They hold the cards so the names cannot be seen and approach another person. Each person says the name of a king or prophet. If a person has that name on a card, it must be given to the other person. After this exchange, each person goes off to repeat the process with someone else. The object is to attempt to collect as many cards as possible of a given king or prophet.

After people have had time to exchange cards, ask for a show of hands of everyone who has two or more cards for a king or prophet. Three or more? Four or more? Congratulate those who collected the most identical cards, then ask them to tell one interesting fact about the king or prophet they collected. If a person is stumped, invite the class to tell something. The real object of the activity turns out to be getting people to recall information about the kings and prophets of Israel and Judah.

CHOICE 2: SIX PERIODS OF BIBLE HISTORY (A REVIEW)

Welcome people as they arrive. Give each person a Post-it Note on which to letter his or her name. Instruct people to browse among the *Bible Time Line* sheets displayed on the wall and select a period when they would have liked to live. They attach their Post-it Note to that point on that *Time Line* page. As people finish this instruction, direct them to ask at least two group members why they chose the time period they did.

After people have had time to post their names and talk to several others in the group, call for volunteers to share the most interesting reasons they heard for selecting a particular point in Bible history.

GETTING STARTED OPTION: (*20 minutes*)
This option will add 10 minutes to the end of the Getting Started section.

Divide the class into two teams (e.g., men vs women, singles vs couples, A-M vs N-Z, etc.). Ask each team in turn the questions in the "Survey Quiz" and those you have prepared. If a team answers incorrectly, allow the other team a chance to answer. If time permits, and the group is still having fun with this "test," invite people to pose questions for the other team. Conclude by inviting the "losers" to applaud the "winners."

GETTING INTO THE WORD

(*40 minutes*)

Step 1—Captivity Under Babylon

Step 2—Restoration Under Persia

Step 3—The Intertestamental Period

STEP 1 — CAPTIVITY UNDER BABYLON
(*15 minutes*)

Remind the class that the kingdom of David and Solomon had been divided and its glory long departed. The northern kingdom of Israel had been led away captive to Assyria in 722 B.C. The southern kingdom of Judah had been spared for 135 more years, finally being taken captive by Nebuchadnezzar, the great king of Babylon.

Explain that Assyria introduced the practice of wholesale deportations of people from defeated nations as a tactic to reduce the chance of rebellion. Other ancient nations, including Babylon, adopted the plan, leaving only the poorest people behind to work the fields and vineyards (2 Kings 24:14; 25:12).

Lead the class in finding the answers to the following questions about the captivity:

What was life like for the captives in Babylon? (Jeremiah 29:4-7—They were able to acquire possessions, conduct business, assemble for worship. Later, when permitted to return to Jerusalem, many chose to stay in Babylon!)

What status did the captives achieve in Babylon? (Daniel 6:1-4—Some captives, such as Daniel, rose to highly influential positions, however there was prejudice and jealousy over such achievements.)

What impact did the captivity have on the spiritual life of the captives? (Ezekiel 33:30-32; Ezra 1:5,6—Ezekiel, who prophesied in Babylon before and after the fall of Jerusalem, continued to call the people to repentance [Ezekiel 14:6; 18:30,32]. Chapters 33–48 envision the return of God's people to Jerusalem coinciding with a changed heart on their part [39:25-29]. When Ezra led a group of returnees from Babylon to Jerusalem, they were described as people "whose heart God had moved" [Ezra 1:5].)

What happened to the Israelites taken captive by Assyria? (There is no record of their return to their homeland. Undoubtedly, some made their way back under the rule of the Persians, but the ten tribes of Israel were never restored. The people who were moved into Israel by the Assyrians became the forbears of the Samaritans, who were hated by the Jews for their mixed ancestry and deviance from orthodox teachings.)

Bible Time Line: page 42 (Daniel)

OPTION (*20 minutes*): This option will add 5 minutes to the Step 1 section.

Point out that two famous prophetic visions were given during this period: Daniel's interpretation of Nebuchadnezzar's dream and Ezekiel's vision of the valley of dry bones. Assign half the class to read about the former in Daniel 2:31-45 while the other half reads Ezekiel 37:1-14.

As people finish their reading, explain briefly that Ezekiel's vision foresaw the national restoration of Israel, while Daniel predicted the succession of four kingdoms: Babylon (the head of gold), Medo-Persia (the chest and arms of silver), Greece (belly and thighs of bronze) and Rome (legs of iron and feet of clay). The final kingdom (the rock) is the eternal Kingdom of God, which supersedes all human governments.

STEP 2 — RESTORATION UNDER PERSIA (15 minutes)

Point out that among the numerous prophecies that God's people would be restored to their land, were remarkably precise predictions of just how and when it would happen. Isaiah 45:13 tells that Cyrus (king of Persia) would "rebuild my city and set my exiles free." Jeremiah 25:11,12 announced that the Babylonian captivity would last for 70 years.

Explain that there were three separate expeditions of captives returning from Babylon. Divide the class into three sections. Assign each section to read brief excerpts about one of these expeditions:

1. Ezra 1:1-8; 3:8-13 (Leader: Zerubbabel—538 B.C.)
2. Ezra 7:1-7; 9:1-4 (Leader: Ezra—458 B.C.)
3. Nehemiah 2:1-6; 4:6-15 (Leader: Nehemiah—445 B.C.)

After people have had time to read their passages, invite volunteers from each section to share a few key points of the events they read about. Expand or clarify as necessary to make sure these facts are shared:

After a few years of rebuilding effort, the first group of returnees (about 50,000 people made this trek) lost their religious fervor and construction on the Temple lagged and then stopped. The prophets Haggai and Zechariah urged the final completion of the work, which was finished in 516 B.C.

It was almost 60 years after the Temple's completion when Ezra led another 7,000 people back to Jerusalem. While Zerubbabel's task had been to rebuild the Temple, Ezra's work was to reform the faith and practice of the people. Ezra's very strong measures taken to end the practice of intermarriage with neighboring peoples is only understood in light of the urgency not to allow Israel to fall back into the idolatrous patterns that had been the root cause of her captivity. After Ezra's reforms, idolatry ceased to plague the religious life of the Jewish people.

Although Nehemiah is famous for rebuilding the walls of Jerusalem, his leadership (in support of the teaching of Ezra) is equally notable for returning the people to a knowledge of God's Word (Nehemiah 8). He also led another reform of sinful practices that had crept back among the people (Nehemiah 13).

Point out that the story in the book of Esther is set in Persia shortly before Ezra's expedition to Jerusalem. Also, the last prophet of the Old Testament, Malachi, probably was a contemporary of Nehemiah. Several of the sins Nehemiah addressed are also condemned by Malachi.

Bible Time Line: pages 43-48 (King Cyrus—Nehemiah)

 OPTION (20 minutes): This option will add 5 minutes to the Step 2 section.

Retain the same three sections of the class and assign each group to read a few selected verses from the three post-exilic prophets:

1. Haggai 2:6-9   3. Malachi 4
2. Zechariah 14:3,4,8,9

 NOTE: If you are completing this session in one meeting, ignore this break and continue with Step 3.

TWO-MEETING TRACK: If you want to spread this session over two meetings, **STOP** here and close in prayer. Inform group members of the content to be covered in your next meeting.

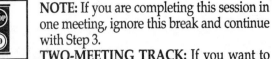 **START OPTION (10 minutes)** Begin your second meeting by leading the class in reading the poem on pages 24 and 25 of *What the Bible Is All About* to review the order and main ideas of the Old Testament books. Encourage people to recite as much of the poem from memory as they can. To assist in this, divide into pairs or trios in which people work together to practice sections of the poem.

Then continue with Step 3 and conclude the session.

STEP 3 — THE INTERTESTAMENTAL PERIOD (10 minutes)

Briefly explain that the 400 years separating Nehemiah and Malachi from Christ were marked by massive changes in the political and social life of the Middle East. Five main ruling dynasties controlled Palestine during these four centuries.

Persian Rule (450-330 B.C.) The Persians continued to control Palestine after the time of Nehemiah, allowing the high priests to carry on all religious observances and to direct local government.

Hellenistic Rule (330-198 B.C.) Alexander the Great not only conquered the Persian Empire, he initiated a vision of the world being unified by Greek culture and language. The Old Testament was later translated into Greek, which became a universal language (Septuagint version). Following Alexander's brief life, his empire was divided among his four generals, and Palestine was under the rule of Ptolemy. During the rule of the Ptolemies, Jews were treated kindly and great numbers of them settled in Egypt and other areas of the Mediterranean world. As Jews were brought into contact with the prevailing culture, they stimulated interest in the Scriptures and an expectation of the coming Messiah.

Seleucid Kings (198-166 B.C.) The Seleucids, a rival Hellenistic dynasty, had controlled Syria and Mesopotamia since the death of Alexander. In 198 B.C., the Seleucid king Antiochus defeated the Ptolemies of Egypt and gained full control of Palestine. At first, the Jews were treated well, but in 175 B.C., Antiochus IV Epiphanes became ruler and launched an aggressive program of forcing Greek culture (Hellenism) on the Jews. The majority

As people complete their reading, remind the class that most of the Old Testament prophets spoke and wrote before the captivity. Daniel and Ezekiel prophesied during the Exile. Haggai, Zechariah and Malachi ministered after the return. (NOTE: Some scholars believe that Joel may have been written after Haggai and Zechariah.)

of Jews were outraged and resisted, triggering a violent response by Antiochus in which 40,000 Jews were killed and the Temple was profaned by sacrificing a pig on its altar and erecting a shrine to Zeus (Jupiter).

Maccabean Independence (166-63 B.C.) One aged Jewish priest, Mattathias, and his family refused to worship any but the true God. A band of Jews gathered around him and his five sons (led by Judas Maccabeus, "the Hammerer"), and soon a terrible insurrection followed. Antiochus attempted to crush this rebellion, but the Seleucids were ultimately defeated during a 24-year war. Sharp divisions over religious matters weakened the Jewish efforts, and power ultimately was taken by an aristocratic, Hellenistic regime (the Hasmonean dynasty), which controlled the priesthood.

Roman Rule (63 B.C. onward) Jewish independence ended when the Roman general Pompey besieged Jerusalem for three months, then massacred the priests and entered the Most Holy Place of the Temple. The Jews were now required to pay yearly tribute to Rome.

Julius Caesar appointed Herod as governor of Galilee, who moved quickly to murder surviving members of the Maccabean family. In an attempt to win the favor of the Jews, Herod promised to build a new Temple, a magnificent structure completed about A.D. 20, 500 years after the second Temple was built under Zerubbabel.

Think of the changes in world kingdoms as God prepared the way for the coming of His Chosen One. Babylon was overthrown. Persia passed away. Alexander's Hellenistic empire rose and fell. Jewish independence flourished and foundered. The Roman republic gave way to an empire under the rule of Augustus Caesar. Finally, the world was at peace. It was the optimum time in all of ancient history for the coming of Christ and the rapid spread of the gospel.

Bible Time Line: page 49 (400 Years—Jesus' Birth)

OPTION (*35 minutes*)
This option will add 25 minutes to the Step 3 section.

THE BLOODLINE OF MESSIAH

Lead the class in this exciting survey to discover that there is one principal subject of the Bible to which every other subject is related. The Bible is Christocentric. Take Christ out of the Old Testament and the whole structure falls apart. The Book, from Genesis to Revelation, has but one theme—the Bible speaks always of Jesus Christ. Paul wrote to the Corinthians, "I resolved to know nothing while I was with you except Jesus Christ and him crucified" (1 Corinthians 2:2). That is the theme of the Bible.

This really is the wonder of the Bible—that it has but one theme, and that theme is the Lord Jesus Christ. Each of the Gospels, which tell the story of His life, take us back into the Old Testament to help us fully understand His mission.

Mark starts his story of Jesus' life by taking us back to the prophet Isaiah: "The beginning of the gospel about

---

Jesus Christ, the Son of God. It is written in Isaiah the prophet: 'I will send my messenger ahead of you, who will prepare your way'" (Mark 1:1,2).

Matthew begins by stating: "A record of the genealogy of Jesus Christ the son of David, the son of Abraham" (Matthew 1:1).

Luke goes further back than Matthew: "He was the son...of Enosh, the son of Seth, the son of Adam, the son of God" (Luke 3:23,38).

John begins, "In the beginning was the Word, and the Word was with God, and the Word was God" (John 1:1).

After His death and resurrection, Jesus explained those events to two disciples by "beginning with Moses and all the Prophets, he explained to them what was said in all the Scriptures concerning himself" (Luke 24:27).

If we open a novel in the middle of the book and begin to read about the hero, we soon find we have to go back to the beginning if we are to understand the story. As you study the New Testament, you quickly find that God's plan of redemption was no afterthought, but it was a clear unfolding of His eternal purpose.

The Old Testament is filled with examples of God working out that purpose in preparation for sending His own Son in human flesh. God's plan was not to redeem humanity by giving us rules or by establishing a philosophy of life, but by living among us in order to become the perfect sacrifice for our sinful rebellions. Thus, one of the most illuminating of all biblical studies is to trace the lineage of the Messiah, discovering along the way, not just a family tree, but an amazing series of incidents that gradually reveal the fullness of God's purpose.

Divide the class into seven groups. Assign each group to read about one segment of "The Bloodline of Messiah":

1. The Human Race of Adam (Genesis 3:15; Luke 3:38; 1 Corinthians 15:45; Hebrews 2:17,18)
2. Preacher of Righteousness, Noah (Genesis 6:5-10; 9:8-13; Luke 3:36; Hebrews 11:7)
3. Father of a Nation, Abraham (Genesis 15:5,6; 18:18,19; Luke 1:72,73)
4. Promised Heir, Isaac (Genesis 21:12; 22:15-18; Galatians 4:28)
5. Branch of Jacob (Genesis 28:1-4; Numbers 24:17-19; Luke 1:33)
6. Tribe of Judah (Genesis 38:13-18,27-29; 49:10; Matthew 1:3; Revelation 5:5)
7. Family of David (2 Samuel 7:16; Psalm 89:35-37; Ezekiel 37:24,25; Matthew 1:1; 12:22,23)

Instruct the groups to look in their assigned verses for clues about the purpose of God as shown by that link in Messiah's lineage.

Allow five to seven minutes for groups to read and talk, then invite a volunteer from each group to report on their findings. Taken as a group, the ancestors of Messiah reflect the full range of human sin and response to God's loving forgiveness.

Summarize this overview of the Old Testament narrative. **The New Testament shows Jesus Christ as the consummation of the bloodline. Jesus is the "son of man," partaking of our nature, dying for our sins, tasting and conquering death on our behalf. As the Son of David, legal son of the royal line, He is coming back to reign, holding dominion "from sea to sea and from the River to the ends of the earth" (Psalm 72:8).**

Notice in Matthew 1:1 Jesus is spoken of as the Son of David and the Son of Abraham. He is not called the Son of any of those who follow those men. Remember, both Abraham and David were specifically promised a son. The immediate fulfillment of that promise to each man was disappointing. Neither Isaac nor Solomon fulfilled the promise of God, but Jesus more than fulfilled it. Both Isaac and Solomon were imperfect. Jesus is perfect. In Him, God's promise is fulfilled.

GETTING PERSONAL *(10 minutes)*

Summarize the fifth period of Bible history (Captivity in Babylon to Christ):

The Greatest Fact: The Restoration of a Remnant
The Greatest Truth: God Mercifully Preserves His People

In spite of continuing rebellion by Israel and opportunistic antagonism by surrounding nations and empires, God patiently repeated His warnings, seeking to turn His people away from their sins. At the same time, He gave frequent messages of hope, first that the exile would end and the Temple be restored in preparation for the coming of Messiah. God's pattern of forgiveness shows, not only in the history of the nation, but in the listing of names of Jesus' ancestors, among whom were adulterers, murderers, prostitutes and idolators.

Encourage each person to think of areas in which they need God's forgiveness. Then lead the class in a prayer of confession. Give an opportunity for any who wish to further explore their relationship with Christ to stay after class or arrange a time to meet individually with you.

OPTION (*15 minutes*)

This option will add 5 minutes to the Getting Personal section.

Show the top of "The Periods of Bible History Outline" transparency as you lead the class in a quick review of the first five periods:

PERIOD	PEOPLE	EVENTS	SCRIPTURE
1. Creation to Call of Abraham	Adam & Eve Noah	1. Creation 2. Fall and Promise 3. Redemption 4. Flood 5. Judgment of Babel	Genesis 1–11
2. Call of Abraham to Coming out of Egypt	Abraham Isaac Jacob Joseph Job	1. Call of Abraham 2. Preparation of Jacob 3. Descent into Egypt	Genesis 12–50 Job 1–42

3. Coming out of Egypt to Coronation of Saul	Moses
	Joshua
	The Judges:
	
	  Deborah
	  Gideon
	  Samson
	  Samuel
		1. Exodus from Egypt
		
		2. Giving of the Law
		
		3. Wilderness Wanderings
		4. Conquest of Canaan
		5. Judges Rule the Land
			Exodus 1–18
			
			Exodus 19–Leviticus
			
			Numbers–Deuteronomy
			Joshua
			Judges–1 Samuel 7

4. Coronation of Saul to Captivity in Babylon	Saul David Solomon Rehoboam Jeroboam Hezekiah Isaiah Jeremiah	1. Kingdom United 2. Kingdom Divided 3. Downfall of the Kingdom	1–2 Samuel 1 Kings 1–11 1 Chronicles 2 Chronicles 1–9 1 Kings 12–2 Kings 23 2 Chronicles 10–35 2 Kings 24, 25 2 Chronicles 36
5. Captivity in Babylon to Christ	Daniel Ezekiel Nebuchadnezzar Ezra Nehemiah Esther	1. Capture Under Babylon 2. Restoration Under Persia 3. Hellenistic Rule 4. Seleucid Kings 5. Maccabean Independence 6. Roman Rule	Ezekiel/Daniel Obadiah Ezra–Esther Haggai–Malachi The Intertestamental Period

Assign class members to read chapters 12-14 in *What the Bible Is All About* or 16-18 in the *Quick Reference Edition*. Encourage them to read the books of Ezra and Nehemiah following the "Selected Bible Reading" suggestions at the end of chapter 12 in *What the Bible Is All About*.

Preview the next session by referring the class to the poem on pages 24-26 of *What the Bible Is All About*. If time permits, take a few minutes to lead the class in reciting the poem up through the end of the Old Testament. Repeating the poem in each class session is an excellent device to help class members learn, not only the sequence of the books of the Bible, but a quick description of the contents of each book.

PERIOD OF CHRIST & THE CHURCH

LOOKING FOR CHRIST'S RETURN

Christ to Consummation of All Things

S·E·S·S·I·O·N · K·E·Y·S

■ KEY VERSE

"For God so loved the world that he gave his one and only Son, that whoever believes in him shall not perish but have eternal life." John 3:16

■ KEY IDEA

God came to earth in human form and suffered because of the world's sins. All of creation awaits the day when He will return and be recognized by all as "King of kings and Lord of lords."

■ KEY RESOURCES

■ Chapters 27-52 in *What the Bible Is All About* and/or chapters 43-72 in *What the Bible Is All About: Quick Reference Edition*

PREPARATION

Provide name tags and felt pens.

Display each of six Period of Bible History posters made for Session 1.

Display pages 1-49 from *The Big Picture Bible Time Line*. Have ready pages 50-68.

Have ready copies of "The Six Mountain Peaks of Bible History" and "The Bible—A Library of Smaller Books" for each person who needs one. Also have ready overhead transparencies of the pages and an overhead projector.

For Choice 1, letter on separate index cards each book of the Bible. Make a duplicate set. Scramble the order of the two sets of cards.

CHRIST'S BLOODLINE

CHRIST'S BIRTH TO HIS RETURN

SESSION 5 AT A GLANCE

SECTION	ONE SESSION PLAN		TWO SESSION PLAN	WHAT YOU'LL DO
Time Schedule	60-85 Minutes	More than 60 Minutes	60 Minutes (each session)	
Getting Started	10	10-20	*Session One:* **20**	Focus on the Big Picture in Scripture
Getting into the Word	40-65	50-75	40	Learn Major Persons and Events of the Period
Step 1	15	20	20	Step 1—The Coming of Christ
Step 2	15	20	20	Step 2—The Church
			Session Two Start Option: **10**	
(Step 3 Option)	(25)	(25)	**25**	(Step 3 Option— Paul's Missionary Journeys/Writings)
Step 4	10	10	10	Step 3—Consummation of all things
Getting Personal	10	10-15	15	Apply Basic Truths to Your Life

S·E·S·S·I·O·N · P·L·A·N

LEADER'S CHOICE

Two-meeting Track: This session is designed to be completed in one 60-85 minute meeting. If you want to extend the session over two meetings and allow group members more time for discussion, **END** your first meeting and **BEGIN** your second meeting at the stop-and-go symbol in the session plan.

The boxes marked with the clock symbol provide optional learning experiences to extend this session over two meetings or to accommodate a session longer than 60-75 minutes.

Mark 1:1,14; 16:19,20
Luke 1:35; 24:36-43
John 1:1,2; 21:5,6,25

Allow two or three minutes for people to look up and read their assigned verses. Then invite volunteers from each section to read aloud their verses and explain what clues they see there. Point out that these brief clues give just a glimpse to themes that are fully developed in reading through the full account. As ideas are shared, be prepared to add information from the "Keys to the Gospels" section on pages 344 and 345 of *What the Bible Is All About*:

Matthew: Presents Jesus as King, the royal Son of David, whose power reaches to the end of the earth.

Mark: Presents Jesus as Servant, continually working to fulfill His Father's mission.

Luke: Presents Jesus as Son of Man, the Ideal, Perfect Human.

John: Presents Jesus as Son of God, united in essence and purpose with the Father.

Point out that the Gospels all focus mainly on the three and one-half years of Jesus' public ministry, starting with His baptism and temptation and ending with His death, resurrection and ascension. In between are the accounts of His teachings and healing ministry. The first three Gospels, Matthew, Mark and Luke, are called the Synoptic Gospels, because, unlike the book of John, they give a synopsis (an overview) of Jesus' total ministry. John focuses on Jesus' ministry in Judea and His deeper and more abstract discourses and conversations with individuals, rather than the public addresses to the multitudes.

There is general, but not complete, agreement by scholars on the main sequence of events in Jesus' ministry. It is very clear that throughout the latter half of His ministry, opposition grew stronger in response to both His popularity and His message.

Read aloud Matthew 21:33-46 in which Jesus tells the second of two parables in response to a challenge by the chief priests and elders demanding to know Jesus' authority for His teachings. This "Parable of the Tenants," which is also told in Mark and Luke (Mark 12:1-12; Luke 20:9-19), vividly summarizes God's patience in dealing with His rebellious people and warns of judgment on those who reject His Son.

Summarize the fulfillment of the Old Testament promise in the Good News of the story of Jesus:

God chose people and symbols and sacrifices to prefigure and predict the character and mission of His Chosen One. In the passover lamb of Exodus 12 we see Christ our passover lamb, whose blood brings redemption when applied to our hearts. We see that, "Just as Moses lifted up the snake in the desert, so the Son of Man must be lifted up" (John 3:14). Jesus is the cure for the snakebite of sin and all the pain and suffering sin has brought to men and women. He is the manna from heaven, the bread of life, the living water. Repeatedly, the story of Jesus echoes and expands the Old Testament message.

Bible Time Line: pages 50-60 (Wise Men—Jesus Appears to Disciples)

OPTION (*20 minutes*)
This option will add 5 minutes to the Step 1 section.

Ask, **What are some ways in which God had prepared the world for the coming of Christ?** List the responses on the chalkboard or an overhead transparency:

- Prophets foretold His coming.
- Captivity in Babylon had cured Israel of idolatry.
- Jews had been scattered throughout the world, carrying their knowledge of God to many cultures.
- The Greek language had become a common tongue across many ethnic barriers, giving wide access to the Old Testament (Septuagint version) and a rich, expressive language for writing the New Testament.
- The Messiah was expected even by people in surrounding pagan nations, called "God-fearing" Gentiles in the book of Acts.
- The traditional religions of the Mediterranean world had been discarded by many, leaving a vacuum ready to be filled.
- Rome had conquered much of the world, creating a stable and safe environment and good roads reaching throughout the empire.

STEP 2—THE CHURCH (*15 minutes*)

Divide the class into six sections, and have people within each section arrange themselves into pairs or trios. Assign each section one significant incident from the book of Acts:

1. Pentecost—Acts 2:1-11,38-41
2. Fellowship, Teaching and Healing—Acts 2:42-47; 5:12-16
3. Choosing Deacons—Acts 5:41—6:7
4. Persecution and Dispersion—Acts 7:54—8:4
5. Conversion of Saul—Acts 9:1-20
6. Good News for Gentiles—Acts 11:1-18

Instruct the pairs and trios to read their assigned passage, then share insights of what those verses reveal about the Early Church.

Allow 5 to 7 minutes for people to read and talk, then invite volunteers from each group to tell the class of one insight they gained from their passage.

Point out that the rest of the book of Acts focuses on the ministry of Paul, describing the dramatic spread of faith in Christ throughout major areas of the Roman Empire. Further insights into the experiences of these rapidly growing churches is provided in the Epistles, letters written to help guide the life of these young congregations. Acts concludes with Paul a prisoner in Rome, but still actively engaged in spreading the Good News. Paul's journeys and writings are explored more thoroughly in the Option section just before Step 3.

Bible Time Line: pages 61-67 (The Ascension—Paul's Shipwreck)

GETTING STARTED (10 minutes)

CHOICE 1: THE BOOKS OF THE BIBLE

Welcome people as they arrive. Divide people into two teams. Distribute among each team one set of scrambled books of the Bible cards. Instruct them to practice putting them in order. People may refer to the Contents page at the front of their Bibles as they practice. After both teams have succeeded in putting their cards in order, ask them to mix up the cards again, then exchange sets of cards with the other team. Give a signal when to begin, and teams compete at putting the cards back in order. When one team says they have finished, lead the class in verifying their work by reading the book names aloud as you hold them up. If you have been learning the poem on pages 24-26 of *What the Bible Is All About*, lead the class in reciting the poem as you or a volunteer hold up the cards.

CHOICE 2: SIX PERIODS OF BIBLE HISTORY (A REVIEW)

Welcome people as they arrive. Invite people to select one of the "Six Periods of Bible History" and stand by that sign. (If you have displayed the *Bible Time Line* pages, they may browse among those.) Encourage people to talk with others who chose that period, helping each other remember the names of major characters who lived during that time.

Allow a few minutes for informal mingling, then explain that you are going to lead them in a brief game to review some of what they have learned. You will call out the names of major Bible characters. The people in the period to which that person belonged must all raise their hands before you can count to five. Anyone who does not raise a hand in time must move to the period to their right. Anyone who raises a hand incorrectly

must move to the period to their left.

After calling at least one name from each period (not in sequential order, of course), you may want to let people huddle with those in their period and choose a name from another period to call out. Besides reviewing characters and their time periods, the object of all this is to encourage people to mingle.

GETING INTO THE WORD (40 minutes)

Step 1—The Coming of Christ

Step 2—The Church

Step 3—(Option) Paul's Missionary Journeys/Writings

Step 4—Consummation of All Things

STEP 1—THE COMING OF CHRIST
(15 minutes)

Explain that the four Gospels ("Gospel" means good story or news) give us four different perspectives on Jesus Christ, far more detailed and trustworthy information than is available on any other person in the ancient world. Divide the class into four sections. Assign a selected opening and closing verse from each Gospel to one section. Ask people to read those verses and look for clues about the unique emphasis of that Gospel writer's portrayal of Jesus.

Matthew 1:1; 28:18-20

GETTING STARTED OPTION: (20 minutes)
This option will add 10 minutes to the end of the Getting Started section.

Show "The Bible—A Library of Smaller Books" transparency. Review the structure of the Bible, showing the cohesion of its central message.

OLD TESTAMENT (39 BOOKS) — AN ACCOUNT OF A NATION
Message: "The Savior Is Coming!"

Law (5 books)
History (12 books)
Poetry (5 books)
Prophecy (17 books: 5 Major Prophets, 12 Minor Prophets)

NEW TESTAMENT (27 BOOKS) — AN ACCOUNT OF A MAN
Message: "The Savior Has Come!"
Gospels (4 books—the Life of Jesus)
History (1 book)

Letters/Epistles (21 books: 9 to churches by Paul, 4 to individuals by Paul, 8 general)
Prophecy (1 book)

The theme of the Bible is "Christ." Everything in the Old Testament points to Him. The Messiah was first promised in Genesis 3:15, for as soon as people sinned, they needed a Savior to redeem them. The Old Testament tells the story of God unfolding and preparing to fulfill that promise.

God saved Noah through whom the Messiah should come. Then God told Abraham that he would be the father of a great nation of whom the Messiah should be born. The prophets kept telling of this Savior—His birth to a virgin, the town of Bethlehem, His demonstration of God's love and compassion, His suffering, even His very words on the cross. His resurrection and Ascension were also foretold many years before His actual appearance on this earth.

The Old Testament is the foundation on which the New Testament is built. The Old Testament gives the history of the Messianic people, the Messianic nation; the New Testament gives the life and the teachings of the Messiah.

OPTION (*20 minutes*)
This option will add 5 minutes to the Step 2 section.
Call for volunteers who will read aloud, without comment, some selected verses about Christ from several of the Epistles.

Romans 3:22-24
Romans 5:1
Romans 5:11
Romans 6:23
Romans 8:34
Romans 8:39
Romans 10:9
Romans 15:18,19
1 Corinthians 2:2-5
1 Corinthians 3:11
1 Corinthians 6:11
1 Corinthians 8:6
1 Corinthians 15:57
2 Corinthians 8:9
2 Corinthians 13:14

NOTE: If you are completing this session in one meeting, ignore this break and continue with Step 3.

TWO-MEETING TRACK: If you want to spread this session over two meetings, **STOP** here and close in prayer. Inform group members of the content to be covered in your next meeting. Invite those who would like to further explore their relationship with you to stay after class or meet you individually during the week.

START OPTION (*10 minutes*) Begin your second meeting by distributing blank index cards to each person. Ask them to write down one question about the Bible that this series has raised for them. Encourage people to share their questions with each other, seeking to find someone in the group who knows the answer. After people have had time to mingle and compare questions, ask for a show of hands of those who found answers to their questions. Invite several to share their questions and answers.

Next, ask for a show of hands of those who have not yet found an answer. Invite several of these to share their questions. Conclude the activity by pointing out that one of the joys and challenges of Bible study is that there is always more to learn. No one has ever resolved all the questions, for in many cases, finding one answer raises additional questions that had not been seen before. Rather than being the final session of discovering *What the Bible Is All About*, hopefully this session will encourage each person to continue investigation into God's Word.

STEP 3 — (OPTION) PAUL'S MISSIONARY JOURNEYS/WRITINGS (*25 minutes*)

Point out that Paul's ministry is recorded in Acts 13-28 and he wrote 13 letters to encourage the leaders and believers in the cities he visited.

Present a brief overview of Paul's missionary journeys, outlining the sections on the chalkboard or overhead as you talk:

1. **First Missionary Journey (Acts 13,14)**
   Sent with Barnabas from Antioch in Syria
   Cyprus
   Antioch in Pisidia
   Iconium, Lystra, Derbe
   Return to Antioch in Syria
   (Jerusalem Council)
2. **Second Missionary Journey (Acts 15:40–18:22)**
   Paul chooses Silas
   Syria and Cilicia
   Derbe and Lystra (Timothy joins)
   Phrygia, Galatia, Troas
   Philippi
   Thessalonica
   Berea
   Athens
   Corinth
   Ephesus
   Caesarea (Jerusalem) Antioch
3. **Third Missionary Journey (Acts 18:23–21:17)**
   Galatia and Phrygia
   Ephesus
   Macedonia and Greece
   Troas
   Ephesus
   Tyre, Caesarea, Jerusalem
4. **Paul's Imprisonments (Acts 21:27–28:31)**
   Jerusalem
   Caesarea
   Voyage to Rome/Shipwreck
   Rome

Point out the following information about Paul's imprisonment:

1. His letters to Ephesus, Philippi, Colossae (the one city to which he wrote that he evidently never visited) and Philemon (a leader in the church at Colossae) are called the Prison Epistles as they were written while in prison in Roman.
2. References in Paul's letters to Timothy and Titus indicate he was released from prison in Rome, and made at least one more missionary journey before being imprisoned in Rome a second time.
3. Tradition says this imprisonment ended with Paul being beheaded.

Divide the class into groups of four. Assign each group one of the cities Paul visited, having them look up the following references in Acts and in the letter Paul wrote to that city. They are to look for insights into the purpose of Paul writing that particular letter to that particular church. Assure the groups that there are no obvious, major connections between the passages in Acts and the verses in the Epistles, but it is helpful to know a little of the background of each church and Paul's experience with them when reading the letters he sent to them.

Rome—Acts 19:21; 28:16,30,31; Romans 1:11-17; 15:18,19
Ephesus—Acts 19:1-12; Ephesians 1:13-17
Colossae—Acts 19:8-12; Colossians 1:3-8; 4:12,13;
   Philemon 1:23
Corinth—Acts 18:1-6; 1 Corinthians 1:10-17; 2:4,5;
   2 Corinthians 12:12
Thessalonica—Acts 17:1-10; 1 Thessalonians 1:4,5
Philippi—Acts 16:22-34; Philippians 1:27—2:7

After the groups have had time to read and talk, invite a volunteer from each group to share any insights they gained about Paul's purpose in writing the letter they considered. Be sure you make people aware that each letter deals with more issues than is revealed in the few brief verses they read.

STEP 4 — CONSUMMATION OF ALL THINGS *(10 minutes)*

Point out that the Church has lived through 20 centuries, has grown in numbers and, in spite of times and areas of setbacks, continues to spread the Good News. Through those centuries into the present, the Church is also waiting for the return of her Lord and Master.

Many places in both the Old and New Testament refer to the final culmination of God's plan for all that He has created. Of these many references, the book of Revelation is the most extensive treatment of events surrounding Christ's return and the establishment of a new heaven and a new earth. Much of the language of Revelation is pictorial, reflecting John's attempt to put in writing the vivid images he saw in the visions given him while in exile on the island of Patmos. Interpreters have long debated the meaning of many parts of Revelation. Without attempting to resolve or even address the areas of disagreement, several passages in Revelation should be part of every believer's understanding of the Bible's message.

Bible Time Line, page 68 (Paul in Rome—John on Patmos)

Read aloud the following verses from Revelation, asking group members to follow along in their Bibles:

Revelation 1:12-18
Revelation 2:3-5
Revelation 3:19,20
Revelation 5:11-14
Revelation 7:9-12
Revelation 7:15-17
Revelation 11:15
Revelation 20:11,12
Revelation 21:1-5
Revelation 22:16,20

Lead the class in prayer, echoing the petition of Revelation 22:20: "Come, Lord Jesus."

GETTING PERSONAL *(10 minutes)*

Summarize the sixth period of Bible history (Christ to Consummation of All Things):

The Greatest Fact: Christ's Coming
The Greatest Truth: God's Sovereign Plan of the Ages

The writer of Hebrews helps us to see the exciting continuity and ultimate victory of God's great plan: "In the past God spoke to our forefathers through the prophets at many times and in various ways, but in these last days he has spoken to us by his Son, whom he appointed heir of all things, and through whom he made the universe. The Son is the radiance of God's glory and the exact representation of his being, sustaining all things by his powerful word. After he had provided purification for sins, he sat down at the right hand of the Majesty in heaven" (Hebrews 1:1-3).

Invite group members to break down into pairs and pray for each other's personal needs, expressing thanks to God for sending His Son. Encourage people to think of specific reasons why they are glad Christ has come into their lives.

Give an opportunity for any who wish to further explore their relationship with Christ to stay after class or arrange a time to meet individually with you.

OPTION *(15 minutes)*
This option will add 5 minutes to the Getting Personal section.

Show the top of "The Periods of Bible History Outline" transparency as you lead the class in a quick review of all the periods:

PERIOD	PEOPLE	EVENTS	SCRIPTURE
1. Creation to Call of Abraham	Adam & Eve Noah	1. Creation 2. Fall and Promise 3. Redemption 4. Flood 5. Judgment of Babel	Genesis 1–11
2. Call of Abraham to Coming out of Egypt	Abraham Isaac Jacob Joseph Job	1. Call of Abraham 2. Preparation of Jacob 3. Descent into Egypt	Genesis 12–50 Job 1–42
3. Coming out of Egypt to Coronation of Saul	Moses Joshua The Judges: Deborah Gideon Samson Samuel	1. Exodus from Egypt 2. Giving of the Law 3. Wilderness Wanderings 4. Conquest of Canaan 5. Judges Rule the Land	Exodus 1–18 Exodus 19–Leviticus Numbers–Deuteronomy Joshua Judges–1 Samuel 7
4. Coronation of Saul to Captivity in Babylon	Saul David Solomon Rehoboam Jeroboam Hezekiah Isaiah Jeremiah	1. Kingdom United 2. Kingdom Divided 3. Downfall of the Kingdom	1–2 Samuel 1 Kings 1–11 1 Chronicles 2 Chronicles 1–9 1 Kings 12–2 Kings 23 2 Chronicles 10–35 2 Kings 24, 25 2 Chronicles 36
5. Captivity in Babylon to Christ	Daniel Ezekiel Nebuchadnezzar Ezra Nehemiah Esther	1. Capture Under Babylon 2. Restoration Under Persia 3. Hellenistic Rule 4. Seleucid Kings 5. Maccabean Independence 6. Roman Rule	Ezekiel/Daniel Obadiah Ezra–Esther Haggai–Malachi The Intertestamental Period
6. Christ to Consummation of All Things	John the Baptist Jesus Christ Twelve Apostles Paul	1. The Coming of Christ 2. The Church 3. Consummation of All Things	Gospels Acts/Epistles Revelation

Encourage class members to read chapters 27-32 in *What the Bible Is All About* or chapters 43-48 in the *Quick Reference Edition*. Also encourage them to read the book of Mark following the "Selected Bible Reading" suggestions at the end of chapter 29 in *What the Bible Is All About*.

If time permits, take a few minutes to lead the class in reciting the poem up through the end of the Old Testament. Distribute the "One-Year Bible Study Plan" sheets and encourage group members to make a commitment to read through the Bible during the coming year, using *What the Bible Is All About* as a study companion.

ONE-YEAR BIBLE STUDY PLAN
LEADER INSTRUCTIONS

The One-Year Bible Study Plan has been designed for these situations:

■ For individual use after participating in a class that used the 5 (or 10) sessions in this manual.

■ For group use when a class wants to follow the sessions in this manual by supporting each other in further Bible study. Group members meet together regularly (e.g., weekly) to share insights and problems from their individual study experiences.

■ For group use when a class wants to survey the Bible over a longer period than 5 or 10 sessions (e.g., one year). The 52 chapters of *What the Bible Is All About* lend themselves to a one-year, once-a-week class schedule. Instead of using the lesson plans in this manual within 5 or 10 sessions, the leader may incorporate the learning activities when appropriate in moving through the scope of Scripture.

As leader, duplicate the Study Plan pages that follow to distribute to your class. (NOTE: There are two separate Study Plan charts, one for people who have *What the Bible Is All About* and the other for those who have the *Quick Reference Edition*.) Duplicate the pages in booklet format so they can be easily inserted inside a Bible or a copy of *What the Bible Is All About*.

When you introduce the One-Year Study Plan to your class, refer to the information on the "Introduction to Study Chart" page to stimulate interest and communicate the value of this Bible Study Plan. If you have never completed such a plan yourself, join the class in committing to follow through on the monthly readings.

You will help your group members get maximum benefit from this plan if you maintain group contact, giving opportunity for people to interact with each other about their questions and insights. If it will not be possible for the group to continue meeting for the duration of the year's study, encourage group members to get started on their own—and the the sooner they start the better.

Should much of the current month already be gone, instruct them to simply make the "First Month" on the chart include the rest of this month and next month. Also, if there are any months in the year (e.g., December) when a person knows his or her schedule may not allow time for continuing the study plan, suggest that month be left off the chart and the name of the following month written in its place. During that "vacation" month, a person may select one or more favorite sections of Scripture (e.g., Psalms, Proverbs, 1 John) in which to do devotional reading until the schedule is back to normal and the study plan can resume. It is better to plan on taking an extra month or two to complete the study than to get discouraged and quit should reading fall behind.

NOTE: If some people have doubts that they will successfully complete the One-Year Bible Study Plan, share a few tips to help them keep going should their determination waver:

1. Tell a friend what you are setting out to do and ask him or her to pray for you and regularly check with you on your progress. Making yourself accountable to someone else will help you maintain your pace and help you apply what you learn.
2. Enlist a friend to join you in the plan. Meeting together regularly to talk and to pray about what you have learned is both beneficial and motivational. Ask God to help you apply one principle you read about each day to your walk with Him.
3. Promise yourself some rewards for completing stages of the plan. You may enjoy anticipating a favorite treat each time you complete a suggested reading goal or all the suggested reading for a month. Also, think of something special to do at the end of three months or six months or the full year. For example, why not plan a "celebration" to which you will invite a few close friends? Invite them out for dinner or dessert and include a brief explanation of some of the benefits you have gained from your Bible reading and prayer.
4. Pray regularly, telling God your doubts about "sticking it out." Ask Him for help in sticking with the daily readings and for help in understanding how He wants you to apply His Word to your life.

Distribute the "What Does The Bible Say About...?" page as an added resource for people who would like to locate some of the key passages on some important topics.

ONE YEAR BIBLE STUDY PLAN
INTRODUCTION TO STUDY CHART

As valuable as a group study is, there is no substitute for systematic, personal Bible study and prayer to grow in your walk with Christ. The plan outlined here will make Bible reading spiritually enriching as well as help deepen your understanding of the Bible both as the history of God's people and as the remarkable unified Book of God's Plan for all humanity. By following this plan, you can read through the Bible in a year, using the helpful guidance contained in *What the Bible Is All About*.

Some people become discouraged in reading the Bible from beginning to end. Some Old Testament sections are difficult to understand and even more difficult to apply to life today. Therefore, this plan lets you spend time each month in three different sections of the Bible: Old Testament Law and History, Old Testament Poetry and Prophecy, and the New Testament. The monthly Bible passages are of similar length rather than trying to complete a book by an arbitrary date. Thus, some pages in *What the Bible Is All About* are listed as resources in more than one month.

This study plan is flexible, giving you some structure and goals, but allowing you to study in the way that fits you best, perhaps even varying your approach throughout the year. For example:

- **Rather than giving daily assignments that may be burdensome, this plan gives monthly guidelines, letting you set the pace.**
- **You may prefer to set aside time every day for Bible study. Or, you might enjoy reading in longer time blocks several times a week.**
- **You might favor the variety that comes by reading from each of the three main sections at each study session. Or, you may elect to complete the month's study of each section separately.**
- **You might want to read the recommended sections of *What the Bible Is All About* before starting to read the Bible portions. Or, you may choose to read the Bible first, and then use *What the Bible Is All About* to help you understand what you have read.**
- **You can decide when to start your study. Keep the chart on the following pages in your Bible or in your copy of *What the Bible Is All About*. As you complete a month's suggested reading, mark the reference on the chart as an indication of your progress.**

What the Bible Is All About: Quick Reference Edition contains three brightly colored bookmarks to aid in keeping your place and marking your progress as you read through your Bible. Or, you can make your own bookmarks.

ONE YEAR BIBLE STUDY PLAN

WHAT THE BIBLE IS ALL ABOUT CHART

▌FIRST MONTH:

OLD TESTAMENT: LAW AND HISTORY
Genesis 1–38 _____   *WTBIAA* pp. 14–40   _____

OLD TESTAMENT: POETRY AND PROPHECY
Job _____   *WTBIAA* pp. 173-185   _____

NEW TESTAMENT
Matthew 1–20 _____   *WTBIAA* pp. 347-360   _____

▌SECOND MONTH:

OLD TESTAMENT: LAW AND HISTORY
Genesis 39–Exodus 25 _____   *WTBIAA* pp. 40-49   _____

OLD TESTAMENT: POETRY AND PROPHECY
Psalms 1–62 _____   *WTBIAA* pp. 187-192   _____

NEW TESTAMENT
Matthew 21–Mark 8 _____   *WTBIAA* pp. 360-376   _____

▌THIRD MONTH:

OLD TESTAMENT: LAW AND HISTORY
Exodus 26–Leviticus 23 _____   *WTBIAA* pp. 49-59   _____

OLD TESTAMENT: POETRY AND PROPHECY
Psalm 63–116 _____   *WTBIAA* pp. 192-193   _____

NEW TESTAMENT
Mark 9–Luke 6 _____   *WTBIAA* pp. 377-389   _____

▌FOURTH MONTH:

OLD TESTAMENT: LAW AND HISTORY
Leviticus 24–Numbers 27 _____   *WTBIAA* pp. 59-72   _____

OLD TESTAMENT: POETRY AND PROPHECY
Psalm 117–Proverbs 18 _____ *WTBIAA* pp. 193-199 _____

NEW TESTAMENT
Luke 7–22 _____ *WTBIAA* pp. 387-391 _____

▌FIFTH MONTH:

OLD TESTAMENT: LAW AND HISTORY
Numbers 28–Deut. 30 _____ *WTBIAA* pp. 72-79 _____

OLD TESTAMENT: POETRY AND PROPHECY
Proverbs 19–Isaiah 7 _____ *WTBIAA* pp. 200-217 _____

NEW TESTAMENT
Luke 23–John 12 _____ *WTBIAA* pp. 392-406 _____

▌SIXTH MONTH:

OLD TESTAMENT: LAW AND HISTORY
Deuteronomy 31–Judges 8 _____ *WTBIAA* pp. 79-106 _____

OLD TESTAMENT: POETRY AND PROPHECY
Isaiah 8–41 _____ *WTBIAA* pp. 217-221 _____

NEW TESTAMENT
John 13–Acts 11 _____ *WTBIAA* pp. 406-424 _____

▌SEVENTH MONTH:

OLD TESTAMENT: LAW AND HISTORY
Judges 9–1 Samuel 22 _____ *WTBIAA* pp. 106-119 _____

OLD TESTAMENT: POETRY AND PROPHECY
Isaiah 42–Jeremiah 5 _____ *WTBIAA* pp. 221-229 _____

NEW TESTAMENT
Acts 12–Romans 1 _____ *WTBIAA* pp. 425-434 _____

▌EIGHTH MONTH:

OLD TESTAMENT: LAW AND HISTORY
1 Samuel 23–1 Kings 2 _____ *WTBIAA* pp. 119-137 _____

OLD TESTAMENT: POETRY AND PROPHECY
Jeremiah 6–36 _____ *WTBIAA* pp. 229-234 _____

NEW TESTAMENT
Romans 2–1 Corinthians 11 _____ *WTBIAA* pp. 434-453 _____

■ NINTH MONTH:

OLD TESTAMENT: LAW AND HISTORY
1 Kings 3–2 Kings 10 _____   *WTBIAA* pp. 137-143   _____

OLD TESTAMENT: POETRY AND PROPHECY
Jeremiah 37–Ezekiel 11 _____   *WTBIAA* pp. 234-253   _____

NEW TESTAMENT
1 Corinthians 12–Ephesians 4 _____   *WTBIAA* pp. 453-487   _____

■ TENTH MONTH:

OLD TESTAMENT: LAW AND HISTORY
2 Kings 11–1 Chronicles 20 _____   *WTBIAA* pp. 143-146   _____

OLD TESTAMENT: POETRY AND PROPHECY
Ezekiel 12–45 _____   *WTBIAA* pp. 253-256   _____

NEW TESTAMENT
Ephesians 5–Titus 3 _____   *WTBIAA* pp. 487-255   _____

■ ELEVENTH MONTH:

OLD TESTAMENT: LAW AND HISTORY
1 Chronicles 21–2 Chronicles 32 _____   *WTBIAA* pp. 145-146   _____

OLD TESTAMENT: POETRY AND PROPHECY
Ezekiel 46–Amos 9 _____   *WTBIAA* pp.257-292   _____

NEW TESTAMENT
Philemon–2 Peter 3 _____   *WTBIAA* pp. 555-607   _____

■ TWELFTH MONTH:

OLD TESTAMENT: LAW AND HISTORY
2 Chronicles 33–Esther 10 _____   *WTBIAA* pp. 146-171   _____

OLD TESTAMENT: POETRY AND PROPHECY
Obadiah 1–Malachi 4 _____   *WTBIAA* pp. 293-334   _____

NEW TESTAMENT
1 John 1–Revelation 22 _____   *WTBIAA* pp. 609-634   _____

ONE YEAR BIBLE STUDY PLAN

WHAT THE BIBLE IS ALL ABOUT: QUICK REFERENCE EDITION CHART

▌FIRST MONTH:

OLD TESTAMENT: LAW AND HISTORY
Genesis 1–38 _____ *QRE* pp. 5-28 _____

OLD TESTAMENT: POETRY AND PROPHECY
Job _____ *QRE* pp. 130-133 _____

NEW TESTAMENT
Matthew 1–20 _____ *QRE* pp. 216-223 _____

▌SECOND MONTH:

OLD TESTAMENT: LAW AND HISTORY
Genesis 39–Exodus 25 _____ *QRE* pp. 28-36 _____

OLD TESTAMENT: POETRY AND PROPHECY
Psalms 1–62 _____ *QRE* pp. 53,134-137 _____

NEW TESTAMENT
Matthew 21–Mark 8 _____ *QRE* pp. 223-229 _____

▌THIRD MONTH:

OLD TESTAMENT: LAW AND HISTORY
Exodus 26–Leviticus 23 _____ *QRE* pp. 36-40 _____

OLD TESTAMENT: POETRY AND PROPHECY
Psalm 63–116 _____ *QRE* pp. 134-137 _____

NEW TESTAMENT
Mark 9–Luke 6 _____ *QRE* pp. 230-234 _____

▌FOURTH MONTH:

OLD TESTAMENT: LAW AND HISTORY
Leviticus 24–Numbers 27 _____ *QRE* pp. 40-48 _____

OLD TESTAMENT: POETRY AND PROPHECY
Psalm 117–Proverbs 18 _____   *QRE* pp. 134-138   _____

NEW TESTAMENT
Luke 7–22 _____   *QRE* pp. 234-243   _____

▌FIFTH MONTH:

OLD TESTAMENT: LAW AND HISTORY
Numbers 28–Deuteronomy 30 _____   *QRE* pp. 56-58   _____

OLD TESTAMENT: POETRY AND PROPHECY
Proverbs 19–Isaiah 7 _____   *QRE* pp. 138-148   _____

NEW TESTAMENT
Luke 23–John 12 _____   *QRE* pp. 243-249   _____

▌SIXTH MONTH:

OLD TESTAMENT: LAW AND HISTORY
Deuteronomy 31–Judges 8 _____   *QRE* pp. 57-67   _____

OLD TESTAMENT: POETRY AND PROPHECY
Isaiah 8–41 _____   *QRE* pp. 148-152   _____

NEW TESTAMENT
John 13–Acts 11 _____   *QRE* pp. 249-257   _____

▌SEVENTH MONTH:

OLD TESTAMENT: LAW AND HISTORY
Judges 9–1 Samuel 22 _____   *QRE* pp. 68-79   _____

OLD TESTAMENT: POETRY AND PROPHECY
Isaiah 42–Jeremiah 5 _____   *QRE* pp. 150-154   _____

NEW TESTAMENT
Acts 12–Romans 1 _____   *QRE* pp. 257-269   _____

▌EIGHTH MONTH:

OLD TESTAMENT: LAW AND HISTORY
1 Samuel 23–1 Kings 2 _____   *QRE* pp. 79-89   _____

OLD TESTAMENT: POETRY AND PROPHECY
Jeremiah 6–36 _____   *QRE* pp. 154-157   _____

NEW TESTAMENT
Romans 2–1 Corinthians 11 _____   *QRE* pp. 268-271   _____

◾ Ninth Month:

Old Testament: Law and History
1 Kings 3–2 Kings 10 _____ *QRE* pp. 89-99 _____

Old Testament: Poetry and Prophecy
Jeremiah 37–Ezekiel 11 _____ *QRE* pp. 155-160 _____

New Testament
1 Corinthians 12–Ephesians 4 _____ *QRE* pp. 270-277 _____

◾ Tenth Month:

Old Testament: Law and History
2 Kings 11–1 Chronicles 20 _____ *QRE* pp. 99-113 _____

Old Testament: Poetry and Prophecy
Ezekiel 12–45 _____ *QRE* pp. 159-161 _____

New Testament
Ephesians 5–Titus 3 _____ *QRE* pp. 276-291 _____

◾ Eleventh Month:

Old Testament: Law and History
1 Chronicles 21–2 Chronicles 32 _____ *QRE* pp. 113-116 _____

Old Testament: Poetry and Prophecy
Ezekiel 46–Amos 9 _____ *QRE* pp. 161-184 _____

New Testament
Philemon–2 Peter 3 _____ *QRE* pp. 292-303 _____

◾ Twelfth Month:

Old Testament: Law and History
2 Chronicles 33–Esther 10 _____ *QRE* pp. 116-129 _____

Old Testament: Poetry and Prophecy
Obadiah 1–Malachi 4 _____ *QRE* pp. 185-215 _____

New Testament
1 John 1–Revelation 22 _____ *QRE* pp. 304-312 _____

GIVING TEENAGERS A BIBLE OVERVIEW

If you are teaching this class to young people, you won't need to make any significant modification in the session plans in this manual, since teenagers were kept in mind when the learning activities were being developed. However, there are a few things to keep in mind in order to make this course most appealing and effective for young people.

1. Provide *The Quick Reference Edition*. This version of *What the Bible Is All About* has proven of high interest to young people with its simple, graphic format. Even those teenagers who rarely read and are unlikely to tackle a book more than one-fourth inch thick, will be instantly drawn into exploring the content of this book.

2. Be prepared for a wide divergence of Bible knowledge among the group members. Some young people may already know all the "basic" Bible stories backward and forward; others may have never heard the names of many major Bible characters. Those who feel they have "heard it all before" may initially feel this course is beneath them. Those who know little about the Bible may be intimidated by the knowledge of others and be reluctant to participate.

- Explain to those who are familiar with Bible content that their knowledge of many of the details will become more meaningful as they gain a sense of the Big Picture.
- Explain to those who are not familiar with Bible content that getting an overview of the book is an excellent way to find how rich the Bible is and all subsequent Bible reading will be far more meaningful as a result.
- Explain to everyone that the issue is not how much Bible information a person knows, but what we do with what we know as we walk with Christ and grow to know Him better.

3. Young people are notoriously shortsighted in their vision of life. Adults often find it hard to communicate with someone who was born after the major events of the adult's life, and who shows little or no interest in hearing about those events. ("You don't remember when Kennedy was shot? You don't remember the Vietnam War? Or the first man on the moon? Where have you been all my life?") This typical lack of concern about things that have happened outside their immediate sphere of reference is a developmental characteristic, not a character flaw. Ultimately, only living through more life experiences will raise their awareness of broader issues and events. In the meantime, the teenager's focus on the here and now poses significant challenges to capture the interest of young people with a survey of Bible highlights.

To capture the interest of young people in this course:

- Share some of your own experience in finding the Bible relevant to contemporary problems (not those of your youth, back in the "olden days,") but those you deal with currently in your family and career.
- Point out that although societies and cultures change, God's plan has remained constant over centuries and across continents. This course deals with the manner in which God has responded to the deepest need of every human heart.
- Ask young people to talk to you about their views of the Bible—and listen with acceptance. Avoid trying to correct their misconceptions at this point. Their reluctance to learn from you will diminish as they sense your willingness to listen to them.
- Select the Getting Started activities (two choices are provided with each lesson) you feel have the greatest appeal to the young people in your class.

ADDITIONAL BIBLE STUDY RESOURCES

What the Bible Is All About is the classic 3 million copy best-seller and takes the reader through the Bible, covering the basics in a simple, understandable way.

What the Bible Is All About: Quick Reference Edition is an easy-to-use Bible handbook and gives a brief overview of the people, events and meaning of every book of the Bible. It includes more than 1,000 illustrations, charts and time lines.

The Big Picture Bible Time Line contains dozens of reproducible pages showing the sequence of events in the Bible.

The Bible Visual Resource Book contains reproducible maps, charts, time lines and graphics for group study handouts or overheads. It includes visuals from *The NIV Study Bible*.

Christ B.C. reveals the Christ who came before Christ—as He was revealed in the Old Testament. Explore and understand how Christ is revealed in Old Testament events, personalities, symbols and prophecies. It will help deepen a relationship with our living Lord. An 8- to 13-week Teacher's Guide for adults is also available.

My Father's Names is a study of the names of God used throughout Scripture. God is called by 80 names in the Bible, such as Shepherd, Father, King and Helper. This inspiring study explores how each name describes an important aspect of God's nature. A companion Group Study Guide is available for an 8- to 12-week group study to be used with the book or the video of the same name.

Walk with Me is a study of the Gospel of Mark. It takes a personal look at Jesus and His ministry. Jesus doesn't ask us to wait until we have our lives all put together before we follow. He asks us to follow Him from where we are right now.

Breaking Through to Spiritual Maturity is a group study based on Dr. Neil Anderson's books, *Victory over the Darkness* and *The Bondage Breaker*. It is a 13-week course, expandable to 24 weeks, and challenges adults to combat the lies of the devil and break free to exciting new levels of growth in Christ.